"Caste, Conversion,
A Colonial Conspiracy"

"Caste, Conversion, A Colonial Conspiracy"

"What Every Hindu and Christian must know about Caste"

Pt Satish K. Sharma

MBCS FRSA

"Caste, Conversion, A Colonial Conspiracy"

Copyright © 2020 by Pt Satish K. Sharma

"The evilest achievement of the colonialist Anglicans during their occupation of India was to condition everyone on the planet to assume that to be born a Hindu meant to be born into a caste."

"The Anglican Colonialist strategy to leverage 'Caste' to deliberately create discord and deconstruct British Occupied Hindu India was hatched on January 4th 1844"

Pt Satish K. Sharma MBCS FRSA

This work is part of an ongoing project to

Dissolve Caste Consciousness.

If you'd like to keep up with the work

Please register for more resources and material at

www.castebomb.com
twitter: @thebritishhindu

Foreword

There are probably more books on the surface of our Mother Earth than at any time in our history and the last thing I had ever wished to do was to add to Her burden. But we live in an age where information is leveraged not just to educate but also to manipulate our capacity to feel and to prepare us before the execution of acts of violence. A world where lies and hate speech are skillfully wielded against the vulnerable and innocent on a scale which would make Goebbels bow in reverence. Words and books are necessary to undo the harm being caused by words and books and so this book has proved necessary.

The 40,000-year-old Hindu civilisation has been the target of colonialist violence ever since Europeans set foot on the DevaBhumi, the land of the Devas. The indigenous Hindu community, whose Dharmic principles of living with the Earth and all of her children demonstrate through direct experience, the falsehood of colonizing "religions", has been the target of unrelenting hate speech for over 1,400 years. This hate propaganda has accelerated in proportion to the appreciation of

Dharmic knowledge systems, by foreigners, knowledge systems such as AyurVeda, YogaVidya and the other 5 Darshanas and in the early years of the 21st Century, the response of the "established by violence" belief systems and institutions has been to attack and vilify at every opportunity.

In 2013, the majority, dominant British Anglican religionists launched a propaganda assault on British Hindus, an assault masquerading as Equality legislation. The intention was simply to permanently establish in law the Colonial trope, the civilizational libel, that Caste is a fundamental principle of Sanatana Dharma and a foundational principle of the Hindu civilization. To establish this in Law ordinarily required community consultation, data and evidence, none of which was conducted or collated and in place of which a campaign of vilification and denigration was deployed. Fortunately, the British Hindu community managed to challenge the defamatory generalization upon which this propaganda was dependent and the assault was defeated. This book is an account of some of the events which occurred and the reports and arguments which were presented to rebut the allegations.

Whilst Hindus globally have been working to erase consciousness of Caste, to return India to its pre-colonial pre-Caste vision of an equitable social organization, Isabel Wilkerson published her magnum opus "Caste" and undid the good work of millions of Hindus in one fell stroke. Her book, which can best be described as a textbook example of confirmation-bias and grossly inadequate research, compounded and fuelled by the "white saviour" colonial complex, manifesting in a person of colour, has harmed the decolonising Hindu family greatly.

This book is not intended to be a work of conventional, academic scholarship (despite being of significantly superior quality to Wilkersons' bestseller, in terms of research) but a text focused on one objective, to be accessible and to educate and empower the unjustly humiliated Hindu and to render apologetic and humble the arrogant "White Saviour Evangelist" Christian.

The facts contained in this book establish beyond doubt the duplicitous influence of the Church of England, the colonial origin of the "Untouchable", and the present-day existence of a Christian lobby intent upon vilifying Hindus in pursuit of their colonialist ideology.

Although this work arose out of the presence of an existential threat to the British Hindu community, its applicability to the challenge faced by Hindus globally must be recognized. The information contained herein, the communications and dialogues which were initiated and the academic, political and religious challenges which were overcome, will help other Hindus face and defeat this anti-Hindu hate campaign, but in a manner consistent with the grace and Dharmic principles which guide us. Those open to learning, irrespective of their "camps", affiliations and inclinations will find value in the contents, those whose vested interests and political prospects require them to dismiss the contents, are beyond reconciliation and will find much to criticize and challenge.

Ultimately, Indians themselves, Hindus and non-Hindus, will have to find a solution to this issue and it is my conviction that the time for the healing of the rift in our Indian family, is at hand. One thing is clear, as will be demonstrated by the contents of this work and that is that non-Indian non-indigenous interlopers in this space, whose interests are served by this conflict, will seek to add fuel to and fan the flames of this conflagration, seeking surreptitiously to perpetuate Caste consciousness - their "good intentions" need to be courteously but firmly ejected.

This issue has been a personal journey of discovery, of reconciling deeply inclusive Dharmic civilizational principles with patently false societal fault lines, of detoxifying colonized accounts of India's history whilst creating spaces free of missionary interference within which to churn facts and philosophy.

The greatest reward has been to witness the impact of this work not only upon Hindu children but on Christian friends who themselves had been conditioned to accept without question the accounts of "Hindu barbarity", constructed, provided and generously proliferated by missionary colonialists. As the world and humanity progress on the traumatic journey of decolonization, the understanding and evidence contained in this work can bring Christians and Hindus, "Dalits" and others together in a manner capable of halting this long-running exercise in colonialist vilification. I am confident that this outcome is inevitable, Dharma, harmony and justice demand it, the only remaining ingredient is momentum and that too is gathering in every former colony.

The research required to produce this work spanned several years, referring to dusty texts sourced in India's pre-Independence back street bookstalls and digging through gigabytes of digital texts and files and I'm immensely grateful to those colonial-era authors such as Mark Twain with his "A Case for India" and Sir Penderel Moon, whose meticulous record-keeping helped me to piece together the pieces of this jigsaw to finally reveal the truth regarding Caste.

I'm grateful to the many who gave encouragement and guidance. I'm grateful to Dr Subramanian Swamyji for his passion for justice and restitution and to Shri Rajiv Malhotraji for his infectious determination and perseverance in the service of Dharma.

I must express my gratitude to my father and mother Harmesh Kumarji and Kanta Raniji whose home and spiritual practices bathed my childhood in dharmic virtues and whose immigrant's stolidity in the face of hateful attacks emerging from racism, prejudice and white supremacy became my inner shield. Their obdurate rejection of discrimination and falsehood seeped into me in childhood and has been the foundation beneath my strength of conviction that this Caste-based vilification of Hindus, must end.

I'm deeply grateful for the support of my family, of my eldest Vivek and Jaspreet, and Varun and Viraaj for their scrutiny, criticism and acceptance of my "absence". Above all, my profound gratitude and respect lie with my dear wife Meena, for accepting what at times must have seemed to be my "Captain Ahab" mission and who despite the mists surrounding this work, and its likely utility, stepped forward to be the tranquillity and reliability which keeps all families moving forward. Her patience and strength were critical and any good that this work may do flows from her support.

In conclusion, as all fabricated un-evidenced colonial accounts of India's history tumble, as we witness the dying days of that marvellous work of atrocity fiction "The Aryan Invasion Theory", its fitting to declare that the Anglican Colonialist strategy to leverage 'Caste' to deliberately create discord and to deconstruct British Occupied Hindu India was hatched on January 4th 1844 and became terminally ill in 2021.

Pt Satish K Sharma,

Langley, Berkshire

20th January 2021.

Table of Contents

❍ What is a Hate Crime?..1

❍ A "Real World" Hate Crime-Scene 3

❍ Introduction 5

❍ The Anatomy of the Hate Crime..8

❍ Who created the Caste System and how?..............................21

❍ Who created the "Dalits"/Untouchables and how?........25

❍ Caste & the Creation of a "Hindu-Odic" Hate Brand 30

❍ The Conversion Agenda and the Threat to
Anglican Expansion..36

❍ Caste, Varna, Jati & Kul..45

❍ The Victims and Casualties of the Lord Harries
Amendment 56

❍ Recognition, Remorse, Reparation and Reconciliation ...61

❍ Conclusions...62

❍ An Appeal to "Dalits" 70

❍ An Appeal to British Christians............................73

O An Appeal to British "Pagans", the Original
Dharmic Community of the UK 76

O An Appeal to Anglican Clergy...78

O Message to Chair, Equalities and Human
Rights Commission (EHRC)...80

O Message to Archbishop Justin Welby,
Lambeth Palace..83

O Bibliography 90

O Appendices 94

What is a Hate Crime?

"The UK Government's plan for tackling hate crime"

July 2016

Hate crime of any kind, directed against any community, race or religion has absolutely no place in our society…. *Rt Hon Amber Judd, Home Secretary*

"Our country thrives precisely because of the rich co-existence of people of different backgrounds, faiths and ethnicities. And that rich co-existence is something we must treasure and strive to protect. Through this action plan, we hope to strengthen that protection over the coming years, to ensure we uphold the shared values that underpin the British way of life.

Hate crime has a particularly harmful effect on its victims, as it seeks to attack an intrinsic part of who they are or who they are perceived to be: their race, religion, sexual orientation, disability or transgender identity.

Hate crimes are pernicious; they send the message that some people deserve to be targeted solely because of who they are or *who they*

1

are believed to be. Such crimes have a deep impact on victims because they are targeted against some intrinsic part of their identity (their race, religion, sexual orientation, disability or transgender identity). Those who commit hate crimes also attack the fundamental values that underpin our diverse society, values of acceptance and respect for others. Through the spread of fear, abuse and violence, hate crime can limit people's opportunities, stopping them from enjoying the full benefits of our society and can lead to isolation and segregation.

Any crime that is motivated by hostility on the grounds of race, religion, sexual orientation, disability or transgender identity can be classed as a hate crime.

There are three categories of hate crime in legislation:

- incitement to hatred offences on the grounds of race, religion or sexual orientation;

- specific racially and religiously motivated criminal offences (such as common assault); and

- provisions for enhanced sentencing where a crime is motivated by race, religion, sexual orientation, disability or transgender identity.

We will only be able to drive down hate crime by tackling the prejudice and intolerance that fuel it. Unless we work to challenge bigotry and to educate young people, hate crime will continue.

https://www.gov.uk/government/news/government-support-for-communities-in-united-drive-against-hate

A "Real World" Hate Crime-Scene

"On the 4th March 2013, in London, a religious fundamentalist, in instigating a process culminating in what can rightly be described, as the most insidious and potentially devastating of hate crimes, placed in jeopardy the life and livelihood of Hindu children. His act threatened to destroy their professional advancement, the rewards of honest endeavour, the spiritual and religious evolution which is the expectation of every Hindu and of many peaceful contented persons, and threatened them their place of respect and dignity in society, indeed the human rights and very well-being of my children, were assaulted by this assailant.

His assault was calculated, it was manipulative and it was premeditated. He chose his location and timing with diligence and his weapon was one which had been carefully precision engineered over many decades, by historically the most violent of religious fundamentalists, and in the use of which he was fully trained.

The hate-crime scene had been set, his co-conspirators were also prepared, having been briefed in the dark corners of the palace, having been given ample opportunity to prepare their own ammunition and choice of weapons and having been briefed on the strategy itself. They too took up their places to both help prepare the minds of the gathering and also to launch their projectiles in support of the impending assault. At a time of tranquillity, in a setting when the assault was least expected, he deployed his lethal projectile and at his signal, his co-conspirators launched their volleys in rapid succession, raining down a hail of hatred upon the wholly unsuspecting victims.

Once the weapon had been deployed and the assault completed, the settling emotional and intellectual dust revealed three casualties – every Hindu ever born (including my children) and yet to be born had been injured, the reputation of all British Hindus lay slaughtered and the dignity and reputation of the institution itself as a seat of "evidence based debate & reasoning" had been, in the eyes of all rational observers, crucified.

The masterful assailant who instigated this act of religious persecution, was Baron Lord Harries of Pentregarth, former Bishop of Oxford, the scene was the British House of Lords and the devastating weapon, a favourite of centuries of Hinduphobics and other spiritually corrosive "assassins of indigenous traditions", was the word 'CASTE'. "

...an account written by a Pt Satish K Sharma, following the House of Lords debate of the 5th March 2013.

Introduction

As is customary these days, before embarking upon any critique, irrespective of how justified, it is appropriate to make a "declaration of innocence", simply to meet the inevitable "ad hominems" and "knee-jerk" uproar which follows, usually from those for whom their own vested interests and prejudices are sacrosanct and for whom evidence is an optional desirable but not a prerequisite.

This note is not an "attack on Christians" but an evidence supported response to the manner in which the primary Anglican Institution, the Church of England has abused its dominant position to architect and inflict a hate crime upon the Dharmic community, Hindus, Sikhs, Jains and other communities of non-Abrahamic Indian origin, resident in the UK.

It is a response to the manner in which Parliament, the Equalities and Human Rights Commission failed in their duty to require evidence and remain impartial, and failed in their duty to protect a non-violent, fully integrated and successful British religious minority, the Dharmic community.

We bear no animosity to Lord Harries the instigator of this hate crime, an elderly member of the Upper Chamber and respected in matters of "Faith & Belief" but in this issue, his actions have had devastating consequences, consequences which we submit were both predictable and anticipated as well as advantageous to an Evangelical Institution committed to the conversion of Dharmic communities, here in the United Kingdom and particularly in their declared target marketplace, India.

We accept that the former Bishop of Oxford was continuing in the culturally "hard wired" tradition of his institutional ancestors (a tradition moulded by a white supremacist Colonial past in which a heaven exists from which Hindus are still barred, an orientation which must be difficult to shed in a single lifetime) a tradition of "religiously colonising and oppressing" my own Dharmic religious ancestors, an activity which if it were not protected by cassocks and crosses, would be a Hate Crime, past and present.

When the Church fathers first encountered the "life – affirming" Dharmic ideals in the India of the 16th/17th century, their own institutions' "life-dominating" ideals were naturally jeopardised and whilst the plunderers set about colonising the physical continent, the Church's missionaries set about their "religious colonisation" of the minds of the Dharmic community. Both employed tactics which fall well within the definition of "Crimes against Humanity" and breach every "Hate Crime" definition being diligently and rightly promoted by

PM Teresa May's government. We submit that the Church of England is still engaged in "religious colonialism" and actively pursuing its mission of "saving the heathen" using the weapons of denigration followed by religious grooming and radicalisation, the deliberate creation of an atmosphere rife, particularly with "Hindu-odium – deep seated hatred of all things Hindu" and thus is actively engaged in Hate Crimes, today.

Religious Colonialism, i.e. the replacement of heathen cultures and religions is as much if not more an act of genocide as the physical genocide, in that it seeks to destroy not only the fabric of a community, but the core psychological links with its ancestors and their spiritual and cultural knowledge. It is an act of emotional and intellectual violence of the most heinous kind, a crime which has no place in the 21st Century, and we petition those responsible for the protection of justice & human rights, to ensure that the Dharmic community of the United Kingdom receives justice and protection from this institution, and its "Caste Proliferation" initiative.

Pt S. K. Sharma, B.Sc (Hons) MBCS FRSA @dharmarising

The Anatomy of the
Hate Crime

O n the 4th March 2013, a debate was underway in the House of Lords, the Upper Chamber of the British Parliament, a debate on the Governments proposals concerning Enterprise and Regulatory Reform Bill, a dry and business like subject, one which hadn't drawn particularly significant interest from outside of the House, but a debate which was well attended and which was important for the Government to see successfully concluded. (Ref Hansard 4th March 2013)

Lord Harries of Pentregarth stood to participate in the debate and introduced what has since become commonly known as the "Lord Harries Caste Amendment". In the hour that followed, in a performance worthy of the best of Shakespearean actors, Lord Harries demanded, pleaded, cajoled and implored the gathered Peers to rush to act and to protect 480,000 of her Majesty's subjects who did not have the protection of the Law and suffered on a daily basis.

Lord Harries demanded that the word Caste be swiftly added to the list of "protected characteristics" already included in the Equality Act of 2010, i.e. Age, Disability, Gender reassignment, Marriage and civil partnership, Pregnancy and maternity, Race, Religion or belief, Sex, and Sexual orientation.

What followed was a masterful nurturing of "Hinduodium" - a passionate hatred for all Hindus, a precise execution of "vilification and denigration by association", co-ordinated with generous helpings of entirely unjustified indignation, self-righteousness and the unrelenting flagellation of the British Hindu community. With manipulation and orchestration worthy of Machiavelli, clothed in cloying false piety, Lord Harries skilfully misrepresented data, which if true, branded 50% i.e. 1 in 2 of all British Hindus, as being guilty of being born prejudiced, perpetrators of discrimination, on a daily basis.

The baton was eagerly taken up by Lord Singh, who, in a remarkable display of prejudice and ignorance, diminished both the Sikh and Hindu traditions by abandoning Satya, "Truthfulness/Reality" in a thinly veiled act of religious persecution. This perfidy was achieved by misrepresenting the fully humanist teachings of the oldest scriptures of humanity, the ancient Vedas. In a speech which brought shame to the memory of the deep ancestral relationship between the Hindus and Sikhs, Lord Inderjit Singh wielded hearsay and religious prejudice itself in connecting Lord Harries' unevidenced, fabricated account of crimes of hatred, directly with the Hindu scriptures. The Honourable Sikh Lord completely avoided the inconvenient truth that over 90% of the cases referred to in the report being contemptuously brandished under his nose by Lord Harries, named his own British Sikh brethren and their British Sikh institutions, as guilty of the self-same charge, an accusation which he was deliberating misdirecting towards the British Hindu community.

The shade of Lord Macaulay bent double in laughter as the epitome of 'Macaulay's children', Honourable Baroness Flather reminisced about her "high caste" Brahmin cook (skilfully sidestepping any explanation of the metric being used to measure "high", as Hinduphobes have always done and continue to do so in the Upper House). She tightened the noose, maliciously and unjustifiably connecting British Hindus to Caste, Dowry Killings and Female foeticide.

In a parade which called longingly to the glory days, when Bible brandishing Anglicans delighted in pouring contempt on Pagans and Heathens alike from their elevated pulpits, Baroness Lady Thornton, who co-sponsored the amendment, pronounced: "Studies confirm the caste system exists in the UK, with over 850,000 people affected", not for a moment feeling the need to consult census data (which records 15,000 British Dalits) or evidence.

Lord Deben called to a mythical imaginary past, populated by those Anglican British saviours who had magnanimously passed legislation to protect non-whites, whilst glossing over the fact that the very need for the legislation was the prevalence of a white supremacist, race-hate filled psyche, one only recently deprived of the benefits of the global "non-white" slave trade and the unrestrained rape of brown and black peoples and nations. A "rose tinted glance" at a period of history which saw Africans being shackled and ferried across oceans in a slave ship named the "Jesus Christ", enterprises which were fuelled and endorsed by the self-same Church whose representative, the former Bishop of Oxford, was that day standing as the saviour of the downtrodden brown folk of India, the so called "Dalit" or "crushed" community.

Lord Harries basked in the glory of being the Saviour to whom the community, whose largely converted Anglican descendants and their Anglican co-religionists, had turned in despair. With arms outstretched, they beseeched his Lordship to free them from the shackles of the notoriously discriminatory British Hindu community with its abhorrent Hindu caste system, and hundreds of their angry community leaders were demanding justice, clamouring at the gates of Parliament that very moment, or so everyone was led to believe.

An honourable Lord of Pakistani Muslim descent, Lord Sheikh launched into a further targeted act of Hindu hatred, whilst completely overlooking his own traditions' ongoing genocide of minority communities, a tradition which has seen Christian, Sikh and most noticeably Hindus, ethnically cleansed in multiple acts of genocide, in both Pakistan and Bangladesh, in even this decade. In the spirit of public service both Lords Deben and Baroness Flather, flamboyantly prideful in their air of Lordly infallibility and supremacy, concluded by pouring scorn and contempt upon democratically elected representatives and the religious leaders of the British Hindu Community.

The remaining Peers bathed in the joy of their most rejuvenating and nourishing pastime, shouldering Kipling's "White Man's Burden" and saving their "new-caught, sullen peoples, half- devil and half-child" the British Hindus, the dark skinned heathen of the 21st Century, from the ravages of their "foreign" uncultured unbridled passions and prejudices.

In a manner reminiscent of the famous "Gungadin", Hindu members of the Lower House led by Labour MP Virendra Sharma and MP Seema Malhotra, a few weeks later regaled their audience with tales of woe and sorrow, tales which inconveniently conflicted with the grass roots experience and personal evidence of many MP's, critically even those like Jon Ashworth of Leicester, from the most Indian of constituencies, and which conflicted also with the community's' own experience of having lived in this country for over 70 years.

Being typical "British Hindus", fully-fledged politically somnambulant members of Aurobindoji's "Hindu Bourgeoisie", the news that the above had happened struck us with the force of the proverbial runaway train.

Lord Harries' assault reached into the very heart of our homes and disrupted the tranquillity of our families and our community, it cast a cloud over our children's future, British children born in places such as Leeds, Ascot and educated in British schools in counties such as Berkshire and Stafford-shire, and fully decent gentle members of our British community. The Church of England through the functioning of the House of Lords, The Upper Chamber of the "Mother of Parliament's" had launched an attack on the British Hindu community.

As members of the British Hindu community which, with only 2% of the population, contributes 6% of GDP, has the second lowest rates of arrest, trial or imprisonment at 0.5% i.e. only 421 Hindus in prison nationally (after British Jews 0.3%) we were stunned to learn of this allegation against us. According to the United Kingdom's Office of National Statistics, of all ethnic minorities in Britain, the British Hindus had the highest rate of economic activity in 2011 whilst suffering disproportionate levels of institutional prejudice and discrimination. Scholars state that the Hindu community in the United Kingdom, and Europe in general, has consistently faced discrimination in immigration policies adopted by the local governments. In local councils, construction or expansion permits for Hindu temples and community centres have been turned down for years, while Muslim mosques and

Christian churches have been approved by the same councils and built. Nearly 50% of Hindu children, both boys and girls, in British schools have reported to being victims of bullying for being Hindu and their religious heritage. Incredibly, 28% of reported Islamophobic Hate Crimes have been now disclosed as crimes perpetrated upon members of Dharmic communities.

To emphasise the level of anti-Hindu discrimination, the recent much publicised Hate Crime Policy, all 40+ pages mentioned the Hindu, Sikh and other non-Abrahamic traditions not a single time, focussing entirely upon the Muslim and Christian communities. Institutional indifference to the suffering of a whole religious community is itself a hate crime, not that the civil servants are the slightest bit concerned about "Casteist Hindus".

All of this and yet, with NO reliable evidence, no social impact analysis, no public consultation and no genuine participation from the targeted minority community – how was it possible that such a Hinduphobic amendment had found its way to the floor of the House of Lords?

The impact of this legislation, the unrestrained hatred towards and denigration of the minority Dharmic religious community and also the torrent of pain being expressed by so called "Dalits", all caused us to stop, dumbfounded in our tracks. A detailed review of the process which climaxed that day in the Lords, uncovered even more deeply troubling and wholly unexpected revelations.

In today's sadly not so Great Britain, a Britain where in 2016

- a Labour Prime Minister, Tony Blair, has been condemned in the strongest of terms for initiating an illegal war, amidst calls for him to be tried as a War Criminal,

- where a Chief Constable is on record as declaring that there are probably in excess of 750,000 paedophiles inflicting incalculable harm upon vulnerable citizens at this very moment,

- where the latest report reveals that in excess of 50% of all girls are sexually harassed in schools

- where surveys have indicated that 1 in 3 of the indigenous British population are racist,

- where we are now on the 4th attempt to conduct an Enquiry into the INSTITUTIONALISED sexual abuse of vulnerable adults and the wholesale grooming of Hindu, Sikh and White young girls spanning a period of 30 years,

- where the Church of England is on record as admitting that it has repeatedly failed to protect vulnerable children entrusted to their care,

- where the Archbishop of Canterbury has accepted that sexual abuse, Bullying, Sexism and Racism are rife and are systemic problems in the "by law established" Church of England,

- where TV Channels are required to seek justice for young men chastised and thrashed until they bled, by evangelical Anglican fundamentalists

- where the latest reports disclose that 7% to 20% of clergy are engaged in abuse.

- where Parliament has been rocked by a succession of scandals concerning abuse and bullying....

... how on Earth was it possible, in the midst of all of these devastating social and religious challenges, with so much work for decent Parliamentarians and Community volunteers to deal with, that the British Hindu community would be been singled out for such generous Parliamentary attention and be targeted for such an insidious corrosive assault?

The Labour Party, the traditional darling of all British Indians, was approached but in response, they deployed the ultimate "weapon of mass compliance" (traditionally very sparingly used as a coercion of last resort, used only to force MP's to toe the party line despite their own assessments). The draconian 3 line Parliamentary Whip itself was summoned to ensure that this legislation was passed, carried on a wave of indignant self-righteousness, without detailed Labour party

scrutiny nor consultation with its Hindu community representatives, and yet there was no reliable evidence to support
the dire need nor the desperate urgency, merely Lord Harries' masterful manipulation of the Parliamentary process.

We British Hindus asked ourselves,

- was it conceivable that such an eminent figure as
  Lord Harries of Pentregarth, had deliberately briefed
  and beguiled fellow Peers with falsified data and accounts, his own religious Institution having already
  groomed them in advance with tales of horror about
  the dreaded British Hindu community and its demonic
  Caste prejudices?

- had he in reality relied on the hope that none of his
  Lordly colleagues would check his data?

- had he judged each of their prejudices and inclinations with such perfection that by pressing the right
  emotional buttons, they could be relied upon to toss
  away all of the long established principles of "unemo-
  tional scrutiny of evidence" demanded of the House
  of Lords, and like a flock of sheep be herded into the
  "Aye" camp, carried on a wave of Hinduphobic revul-
  sion and unbridled condescension?

- Was it possible that Lord Harries, like his philosophical predecessor, Matthew Hopkins, the WitchFinder
  General of East Anglia whose job was to find, hunt and

burn witches, was intent on seeing evil where none existed, purely to protect and resurrect the crumbling ideology of a Church in crisis? A fundamental skill in the WitchFinder Generals repertoire was to create an air of suspicion and hatred towards any wise woman who had the temerity to question the nonsense which was being peddled by the medieval Church, so much so that when her trial occurred, her guilt had already been established in the minds of her own community; a leveraging of human emotional irrationality which occurred with such frequency that it became a legal principle in its own right, the principle of the infamous "crimen exceptum" and which resulted in an instinctive institutional mistrust of women, existent in the Church to this day. Was this possible?

- Would it be too cynical to suggest that this was merely the latest in a long tradition of denigration of the oldest, non-violent spiritual tradition, by Bishops belonging to the Institution which gave moral and religious authority to the white supremacist atrocities of the genocidal Anglican Colonialists, the world over less than a century ago?

The famous Anglican fundamentalist Wilberforce, in 1813 addressed the same Parliament, in the Commons saying "Our religion is sublime, pure and beneficent, theirs (the Hindus) is mean, licentious and cruel" whilst James Canning standing tall on the Anglicans belief in their own superiority, told a gathering of Hindus "You are all a parcel of poor ignorant semi barbarians, you do not even understand your own language and system as well as we enlightened Englishmen who have been at regular Grammar schools.." all whilst Bishop Heber was crafting a hymn chanting ..

"The heathen in his blindness, bows down to wood and stone... can we whose souls are lighted with wisdom from on high, can we to men benighted, the lamp of life deny"? Judging from the words of Lord Deben, one has to ask whether the "white supremacist orientation of old" of the House of Lords, with its assumed superiority over even grass roots heathen community organisations, is still alive and well, thriving and active, covertly if not overtly. Has so little changed in the Upper chamber in over 200 years?

We reflected upon the number of times in history that the Church of England had filled the minds and hearts of the innocent British peoples, subjecting them to stories of "sullen peoples, half-devil and half-child" witchdoctor bogeymen, and then simultaneously fanning the flames of prejudice, sympathy and anti-Hindu hatred, whenever funds or favour were required? Many now feel that there is more evidence for the present existence of this attitude as an active policy of Lambeth Palace, than there is supporting the entirely divisive and intrinsically prejudiced "Lord Harries' Caste amendment".

What had occurred was perfectly described in "Racism without the Racists" (Bonilla-Silva, page 41) in remarking "When cultural racism is used in combination with the "minimization of racism" frame, the results are ideologically deadly". We submit that this was the intention.

Prime Minister May meeting the traditionally hereditary, hierarchical, endogamous i.e. Casteist British Royal Family.

Who created the Caste System and how?

We wondered about the consequences to Hindu Christian InterFaith dialogue when it became common knowledge, that the Caste system which Lord Harries was railing about, was itself a creation and imposition of white Anglican Colonialist missionaries. There were indeed then, as now a very small minority of decent men and women who abhorred their own creation seeing its destructive effect, whilst continuing to impose it, but history is clear that the overwhelming majority of Anglican Clergy revelled in its effectiveness when it came to deconstructing an integrated and robust indigenous culture and society, softening its vulnerable psychological underbelly, ripe for the stab of a supremacist evangelist's missionary thrust.

The Lords did not refer to the annotation made by the white Anglican ML Middleton *"We pigeon holed everyone by caste and if we could not find a true caste for them, labelled them with the name of hereditary occupation. We deplore the caste system and its effect on social and economic problems, but we are largely responsible for the system we deplore. ML Middleton, ICS, Superintendent of the Government of India, in the Census 1911 Report for Punjab and Delhi (Vol. 15, Part I, p. 343)."*

Lord Harries, former Bishop of Oxford, graced with the mantle of academic rigour associated with a Dean of Kings College, moulded in scholarship by Selwyn College Cambridge, and a Gresham Professor of Divinity, can be expected to know what most informed Hindus know, that amongst the educated Hindus it is accepted that the Anglican plunderers, known romantically as "Colonialists", created what is referred to as the modern day caste system in India. In doing so in India, the social engineers of the Anglican Church were recreating the horrific power structures which they, as the religious and moral force in Victorian Britain, had also created in Britain and successfully inflicted upon the British population in the 18th and 19th centuries.

And here in the 21st Century, an Anglican Bishop supported by a post-colonial establishment was once again, blackening whole swathes of a minority British community, using the same philosophy, only this time he was bringing home one of Colonialist Britain's most successful exports, the concept, the trope and ideology of Caste.

Even Wendy Doniger (hardly a friend of Hindus) also asserts that the British colonial administration nourished and sustained the caste system because it echoed the subtle and deeply entrenched social hierarchy already prevalent among the British themselves. Subsequently, the colonial state deliberately raised the caste consciousness of the sepoys of the Bengal army, manipulating Brahmins and Jats both to regard themselves as elite and to become more particular about jati principles such as the preparation and eating of their food. Doniger has noted that the notions of caste, which in India had traditionally been relatively fluid and secondary, became rigid because the sepoys were made to understand caste as being central to their notions of self- identity and respect. "Subsequently, the idea that the caste is the basis of the Indian social order and that to be a Hindu is to be a member of a caste became a dominant colonial axiom" (Doniger 2009).

Dr Shashi Tharoor, former Under-Secretary General to the UN, in his book "Inglorious Empire – What the British did to India", writes "The British however promulgated the theory that Caste Heirarchy and discrimination influenced the workings of Indian Society. This is arguably a very narrow definition of how Indian Society actually functioned in the pre-British era, and it is thanks to colonial rule that it has now become conventional wisdom." Tharoor continues to quote Dirks' "seminal work - Castes of Mind" in saying "it was under the British that caste became a single term capable of expressing, organizing and above all systematizing India's diverse forms of social identity, community and organisation. As a result of a concrete encounter with colonial modernity during two hundred years of British domination… colonialism made caste into what it is today."

History, no doubt inconveniently for the British (and especially for the moral and religious guiding hand behind the depredations of the Raj, the Anglican Church of England) establishes clearly and irrefutably that the responsibility for the horrors of Caste lies at the gates of Lambeth Palace. After all if they were not at all connected with the moral values prevalent then (and now) what function do they perform for which they receive exemption from taxation, access to the public purse and automatic influence in the law making process of the nation?

The answer to the question "who created the Caste system?" is that the missionaries, Anglican Jihadis of the British Raj, with their headquarters in Lambeth Palace, blessed by the Archbishop and Bishops of the time, created the Caste system as an intrinsic element of their 19th century Census activities and colonialist, evangelical mission. The Church of England is responsible and to be held accountable for the creation of the Caste ideology in the context of India and for today trying to impose it yet again on Hindu citizens of Great Britain.

Who created the "Dalits" / Untouchables and how?

T he Honourable Lords avoided mention of the policy established by Lord Elphinstone, which he trumpeted in saying "Divide and rule (Divide et Impera) was the Roman motto and it should be ours" and Lord Deben avoided mention of the British creation of legal instruments such as the "Criminal Tribes Act" of 1871 which labelled whole communities of Hindus as being "Guilty at BIRTH", in precisely the same manner as Lord Harries' amendment seeks to do today, 145 years later.

James Fitzjames Stephen, another honourable Parlia-mentarian addressing the House in 1871 noted, "people from time immemorial have been pursuing the caste system defined job- positions: weaving, carpentry and such were hereditary jobs. So there must have been hereditary criminals also who pursued their forefathers' profession." On another occasion defining his theory he commented, "When we speak of professional criminals, we...(mean) a tribe whose ancestors were criminals from time immemorial, who are themselves destined by the usage of caste to commit crime, and whose descendants will be offenders against the law, until the whole tribe is exterminated".

When the Anglican white supremacists of the Raj arrived in India, of the 540 principalities existent at that time, over 400 were ruled by Shudra Kings (Professor Vaidyanathan, IIM Bangalore). When the British left, the second largest landowner in India after the Indian Government, was the Church and thus it's reasonable to note that the largest transfer of assets and land from was in fact from the Shudra groups (Lord Harries' so called low-castes) to the Church. Further, there is readily available overwhelming historical evidence that the Dalits "the Untouchables" were themselves a creation of the crushing sanctions created and imposed by the Anglican Colonialists of the Church of England as is clarified below.

The castes and tribes "notified" under the 1871 Act were labelled as Criminal Tribes for their so-called "criminal tendencies". As a result, anyone born in these communities across the country was presumed a "born criminal", irrespective of their criminal precedents. This gave the British Colonial police sweeping powers to arrest them, control them, and monitor their movements. Once a tribe was officially notified, its members had no recourse to repeal such notices under the judicial system. From then on, their movements were monitored through a system of compulsory registration and passes, which specified where the holders could travel and reside, and district magistrates were required to maintain records of all such people. However, when they tried to make a living like everybody else, they did not find work outside the settlement because of public prejudice and ostracisation and this has continued to this day. The British rulers enforced this law for almost 80 years, with the determination, meticulous attention to detail and diligence which has become the hallmark of "Britishness" with vast numbers being removed from their ancestral communities and culture and being marginalised in society, forced to live in "reservations" on the outskirts of towns and villages. Denied all other livelihood they resorted to scavenging and performing the most degrading tasks such as sewage workers and tanners. Madras alone saw 273 tribes being grouped as "criminal by birth" in one fell swoop of the British Legislators pen.

When India gained freedom from the British in 1947, when Lord Harries was 11 years old, thirteen million people in 127 "criminal by birth" communities faced search and arrest if any member of the group was found outside the area prescribed to them, by Anglicans.

This was the genesis of the Dalit or "untouchable". This masterfully destructive British legislation of 1871, precisely like the Lord Harries' amendment, was posed widely as a social reform measure, which reformed "by-birth criminals" through work. The Colonial white supremacist agents of the Church of England created the "Untouchable Caste" and today wring their hands in shared compassion and solidarity with the self-same "Dalits", supporting them in their hour of need, against the terrible wrongs done to them by those demonic Brahmins, those educated Hindus who had the temerity to challenge the predator priests of the Church of England, then and now. The Shudras and tribes challenged the British with physical force and were crushed to become the downtrodden, the Brahmins challenged the Anglicans with knowledge and religious spiritual wisdom and were vilified and denigrated and portrayed globally, as the oppressors of the Dalits, "divide et impera"… divide and rule.

It beggars belief that decades later we are still hearing the same reasoning from luminaries such as Lord Harries, and yet almost all of the British establishment are quite happy to accept without scrutiny, the reasonableness of what is being proposed. This implies that even today it's perfectly natural to assume that such reasoning only applies to "brown non-Christian folk". If "criminal- by-birth" were universally applicable, the present-day white Christian descendants of the Slave Traders and Colonialists, almost all of European "nobility" and certainly the Bishops of the Upper Chamber, are guilty of crimes against humanity on such a scale that a whole continent would have to be converted into prisons to contain all of them.

The horrors inflicted upon Hindus by the conversionary missionary strategies and bumbling social experimentation of the Anglican invaders were so grave that when Emily Eden arrived in India accompanying another agent of cultural genocide, Lord Auckland, she wrote back to her relatives in England "I wonder how we are allowed to keep this country a week …. Why don't they cut all our heads off and say nothing about it?" A slightly different observation to the self-deluding remarks made by Archbishop Rowan in 2007 when he remarked that the "British experiment in India was an example of caring colonialism".

The answer to the question "who created the "Dalits/ Untouchables" is that the Anglican Missionaries and their agents of the British Raj, created the Dalits/Untouchables in the Anglican "concentration camps" under the authority of the Criminal Tribes Act of 1871.

Today's Dalits are the descendants of those who survived the horrors and degradation of the Anglican concentration camps. The Church of England is morally and legally responsible for these concentration camps and the ensuing 140 years of "crimes against humanity" targeted at Hindus and especially Hindu Dalits, and must now be held accountable.

Caste & the Creation of a "Hindu-Odic" Hate Brand

Hinduphobia is an inadequate word since no-one has an irrational fear of Hindus, but a precise word is needed to describe the manner in which hatred of Hindus has been instigated and the flames of Hindu hatred fanned, an air of contempt for Hindus so carefully nurtured. Using a Latin word to convey a degree of academic or religious grandeur is in keeping with the occidental traditions and the word Odium ie "general or widespread loathing and hatred" is a better descriptor for the ideology and process being presented. Hinduodium - i.e. "general or widespread loathing and hatred of Hindus"

The Right Honourable Lords further ignored the manner in which the evangelical Church has carefully and diligently developed the word "Caste" into the global, ultimate anti-Hindu, Hinduphobic, "Hinduodic" brand, the use of which can be relied upon to instantaneously trigger hatred and fear of Hindus – it was crafted with this purpose in mind by Anglican missionaries and is knowingly and unknowingly leveraged by them to this day. It is now a trigger word, a word which can, like "n***er", "paki", "chink" and "wog" before it, be relied upon with Pavlovian predictability, to create feelings of contempt for all things non-white, foreign, Hindu or Indian, so much so that, like all advertising brands the faculties of thought, reason and the need for supporting evidence, are not even considered necessary or even relevant. The falsehood of Caste has become an assumed truth – i.e. a Hindu phobic, hindu odic prejudice, a classic trope.

As evidence of this pinnacle of the achievements of the su-premacist Anglican clergy, we submit the following incident which occurred as recently as 29th May 2016 and which was broadcast upon the BBC's national television channel BBC1 and in which the NCHT's own General Secretary, Pt. Satish K Sharma, was participating as a Hindu representative. The sub-ject of this TV programme was "Did Man Create God?" and as one can rightly assume, Caste has no relevance and should never even have entered the course of the dialogue. The reality was however starkly different; when Pt Sharma was receiving a degree of audience support for the Hindu view, the host Nicky Campbell true to his no doubt unconscious condition-ing, immediately interjected "But you Hindus have the Caste system"… again the principle of the Pavlovian dogs at work, because as everyone knows, "Hindu" automatically equates with Caste. Unconscious conditioning is the most favoured weapon of the supremacist racist and we could almost hear the Bishops in their gilded Palaces clapping their hands with delight.

Relying upon the unquestioning acceptance of this "hate crime" brand, and certain that the same Pavlovian forces and principles would to be effective and available to him on the 4th of March 2013, Lord Harries transformed the Upper Chamber of the British Parliament, the House of Lords itself, into British Shimla, the summer retreat of choice of the plundering pirates of the Anglican Raj. Kaye writing about Shimla in 1851 recalls "that pleasant hill sanatorium, where our Governor General, surrounded by irresponsible advisers, settles the destinies of empires without the aid of their legitimate fellow counsellors, and which has been the cradle of more political insanity than any within the limits of Hindustan"….. Listening to Lord Deben's speech on that spring day in March, one can't help but be thrown back into memory, to the balmy, good old days of the Shimla hill station, mem sahibs and the glorious Raj. Whilst listening to Lord Deben wax lyrical about the tradition of British values another memory also springs to mind when in 1857, the Governor-General Lord Canning another devout Anglican, wrote to a British official :

"As we must rule 150 millions of people by a handful (more or less small) of Englishmen, let us do it in the manner best calculated to leave them divided …… and to inspire them with the greatest possible awe of our power and with the least possible suspicion of our motives." Anglican Interfaith at its finest.

Noteworthy is the fact that devout Christians had equally successfully applied this policy in the New World. According to one 1859 account, the native proverb that the "white man spoke with a forked tongue" originated as a result of the colonialists tactic, in their war with the <u>Iroquois</u>, of inviting their enemies to attend a Peace Conference, only to be slaughtered or captured 16.

Returning to the present, and scrutinising the alleged solution itself in more detail, any rational unconditioned academic or government legislator (assuming one such can be found in this non- secular establishment) would understand that the enshrining in Equality law, which details as protected characteristics, non-hierarchical, naturally occurring, involuntary attributes such as colour and gender etc, of a hierarchical social man made construct, is unquestionably a mechanism for the destruction of the very fabric of any harmoniously cohesive interfaith society, a society to which we British Hindus fully aspire in this Great Britain, our home. Even more so when the construct is an Anglican instrument of colonial cultural and social genocide of the indigenous people of India.

Upon further inspection of the solution suggested by the honourable Lord Harries, it becomes clear that in profile and policy, this amendment to the Equality legislation is consistent with the very contemporary profit motivated tradition adopted in almost commercial frauds. Take for example pharmaceutical frauds such as Vioxx etc. i.e. peddle a solution which on the surface appears to deal with the symptoms whilst leaving the root cause carefully untouched, generating a future revenue stream to be harvested for decades to come. The "ayurvedic" holistic solution would be to grasp the very root and either negate its action or even better, to wrench it out once and for all, allowing the body to heal from the flow of natural energies of wellness and life. This is an approach the Dharmic community has adopted in re-establishing itself here in the UK, having wrenched out the caste memetic virus, becoming "caste free" and the evidence of our Dharmic children's harmonious coexistence proves that it has worked successfully, so much so that the Bishops have evidently been moved to re-launch such a desperate strategy.

In the Caste Clause scenario, architecting a genuine solution also requires that we recognise that the Anglican Bishops do not have what legal tradition calls "clean hands" and that since they themselves initially infected the Indian psyche with this evil mental virus, for purely political and monetary gains, it's unlikely that their contribution at this time will be in the interests of British Hindus or Indian Hindus nor indeed the interests of the wider multi-faith British community. It is also pertinent to note that the complete ascendency of the Anglican theocracy in India was thwarted by the sustained challenge presented by the Hindu intellectuals, the philosophers and the spiritual teachers (known as Brahmins), the natural foe of the aggressive proselytising missionaries and this remains the case, to this day.

To avoid any shred of doubt, this law seeks to make hate speech against Hindus, Sikhs and Jains, i.e. Dharmic religions, the law of the land, in precisely the same manner as was so effectively implemented by the colonial Anglicans in India as their legacy, a parting gift of the Anglican "Jihadis" of the Raj. The Church of England is both responsible and accountable.

The British forced a caste system on India, blamed the Hindus and then sent hordes of Missionaries to "help" them get rid of it ..... meanwhile in England

HEREDITARY
HEIRARCHICAL
PRIVELEGE

THE BRITISH

CASTE

SYSTEM
ALIVE AND
KNEELING

The Conversion Agenda and the Threat to Anglican Expansion

T he fundamentalists of the Anglican tradition are at this very instant, fully engaged in grooming and radicalising the least educated and most vulnerable, sowing discord and creating an "army of the discontented" in India and now it would seem, here in the Britain of the 21st Century.

Archbishop Justin Welby trumpeted his desire to concentrate upon Evangelism, which to non- Anglicans and indigenous cultures means "grooming in preparation for radicalisation". The most despicable but wholly critical and vital aspect of this strategy, includes repeatedly blaming the "high castes" for the poverty in India, ignoring all of the evidence which indicates that over 40 TRILLION POUNDS of wealth was the monetary harm to India, during and since the heady days of the Anglican jihad.

It should be further noted that the maximum number of conversions has been amongst the least educated and least knowledgeable and also the most innocent and most vulnerable and these are the peoples who are even today being groomed and radicalised by the Christian proselytisers in India's hospitals and schools and other places where vulnerable desperate souls can be coerced and converted. Even a cursory inspection reveals the favoured strategy of the white supremacist plunderer at work, "Divide et Impera", divide and rule, in full flow and being sustained by the present day Church of England.

There is one key fact which the Hinduodic manipulators of Lambeth Palace rapidly skip, hoping that no one will ever ask....... What is the metric by which a Hindoo was classified as high caste or low caste? It wasn't money, the Brahmins were always traditionally poor having taken a vow of simplicity, it wasn't political power or land because when the Anglican plunderers arrived in India, two thirds of the country was ruled by Shudra kings and Queens, like the famous devotee of Paramahansa Ramakrishna, Rani Rajmohini of Kolkata. So what metric was used to denote whether a person was "High" or "Low"? There is only one metric which applies consistently to every occurrence of "caste measurement" and that is simply this .... the threat level to the Church of England. The educated spiritual priests and intellectuals were all banded together into one and labelled "highest caste" because they represented the "highest threat" to Anglican domination and those who represented the "lowest threat" to the

Anglican jihadis were pushed into the lowest caste. It then became a simple task of applying the "civilisational asset strippers" weapon of cultural genocide "divide et impera" and the rest, as they say is history.

The Colonialist Anglicans having built their religious empire in Britain by leveraging physical force and fear, found in India religious ideas which, if shared with their flock, would reveal the shallow emotional and intellectual manipulation of the Church's ideology. They discovered, like thousands of pilgrims to India before them, teachings and wisdom which celebrated and elevated humanity as inherently and intrinsically, divine and not sinful. They found concepts which applauded exuberant human creativity and ingenuity and which above all, worshipped as divine, the human sibling faculties of "jnana" and "bhakti", wisdom and devotion, in a unique union, a wholeness of blissful tranquillity, a natural state called Yoga. They found teachings which celebrated and elevated the Divine Feminine and gave equality of status to women in all matters, established and protected with the power of religious sanction. To this day Hindu Temples in every corner of the world celebrate the Devine Feminine and the Divine masculine, as equal.

The late Huh Shih, nationalist scholar, diplomat and one of the legendary leaders of Chinese thought, in a paper presented at the Harvard Tercentenary Conference of Arts and Science in 1936, made a fundamental observation on India's contribution to the evolution of Chinese civilisation.

"India", argued Huh, "conquered and dominated China culturally for two thousand years without ever having to send a single soldier across the border.... Never before had China seen a religion so rich in imagery, so beautiful and captivating in ritualism and so bold in cosmological and metaphysical speculations. Like a poor beggar suddenly halting before a magnificent storehouse of precious stones of dazzling brilliancy and splendour, China was overwhelmed, baffled and overjoyed. She begged and borrowed freely from this munificent giver...China's indebtedness to India can never be fully told."

Fearing a similar fate, the Anglican Church fathers however adopted a different approach. Selecting a pathology most akin to cancer, they attacked the physical, spiritual, academic and linguistic organs of the civilisation, with a truly British level of meticulous determination. Had they applied the same effort to understanding Hindu teachings with love and honesty, the world would have seen a global evolutionary leap of all of humanity. The price to be paid for such a leap, being the death and possible resurrection of the Church of Empire, was deemed too high. Seeing this dire threat to their multi-national, transgenerational religious land grabbing "Ponzi" scheme, they set about the deconstruction of the very being of India and chose a path of destruction of the best of all things human.

And now, woe of all woes, those heathen followers of Dharmic traditions, in all of their ebullient variety and diversity, had found their way to the shores of Britain, and started living and sharing this vision of a blissful tranquil interfaith union. The threat level was detected as "high" and the Caste legislation strategy brought back to its philosophical home. Honourable Lord Deben was only partly correct when he stated "If there is one thing that really annoys people about immigration, it is when people bring to this country, attitudes that are wholly contrary to the traditions of Britain". We would suggest to Lord Deben that Caste is very much a British ANGLICAN tradition, as British as Colonialism itself.

This legislation is a deliberate assault on all British Hindus, Sikhs and Jains and in its spirit and purpose is identical to that social manipulation so skilfully wielded by the Anglican profiteers of the days of the "Raj". Durant in 1930 writes "The British Conquest of India was the invasion of and destruction of a high civilisation by a trading company utterly without scruple or principle, careless of art and greedy of gain, over-running with fire and sword a country temporarily disordered and helpless, bribing and murdering, annexing and stealing, and beginning that career of illegal and legal plunder which has now gone on for one hundred and seventy three years, and goes on at this moment while in our secure comfort, we write and read." It is noteworthy that the moral and religious sanction of the Church of England was very much present in every shade of the above devastation and desecration, a period in which the Church of England too, filled its coffers with blood stained plunder, and the same spirit of societal corruption is worryingly evident in this Church of England

inspired, Lambeth Palace endorsed, Bishop Lord Harries'
"Caste Amendment".

To avoid any shred of doubt, this law seeks to make hate
speech against Hindus, Sikhs, Jains and Hinduism, the law of
the land, in precisely the same manner as was so effectively
implemented by the colonial Anglicans in India as their legacy, a parting gift of the Anglican jihadis.

Sustained denigration of all Hindu scholars, priests and
educated families and guilds was as critical to the success
of this cancerous assault as was undermining the Dharmic
teachings themselves and Anglican scholars did this by deliberately conflating and mistranslating texts that had been
unchanged for over 4 thousand years. Suddenly the fluid,
supportive empowering social structures which had created
the greatest, most harmonious and unwarlike civilisation,
were gleefully misrepresented as vehicles for social injustice, sustainers of discrimination and oppression. Western
scholars and historians like Arnold J Toynbee and Will Durant have written that Hinduism represents the oldest wisdom known to humanity and is the mother of all religions
in the world. It has been well said that the "gentle wisdom
and learning" tradition of Hinduism supported and nourished the world, at a time when divisions of humanity on
the basis of "Religion & Belief" were non-existent. This was
the Hinduism the Anglican missionaries found when they
arrived in India. This is the Hinduism Lord Harries is fearful
of today.

The interest in Caste of the conversion obsessed missionaries, as we have seen, is not a new phenomenon. On 4th January 1844, in colonial Madras, Rev Joseph Roberts of the Royal Asiatic Society of Great Britain addressed a gathering of lead missionaries of the various Churches. He began his address as follows:-

> *In consequence of very strong opinions recently put forth in a Madras publication respecting Caste in the Church, and the sentiments still entertained by some Christians as to its character and toleration; the determined adherence of numerous native members to this system, in the various duties of life; and the solemn fact that next to the love of sin, Caste is the great barrier betwixt the Pagans and Christ, I have thought it advisable to call your attention to this difficult and painful subject...*

Roberts then proceeds to speak of its probable historical source but remarkably refers to Caste as follows – *we think however that this wonderful institution of India, merging in the wisdom and craft of man ...* and then he describes at length the benefits of this OCCUPATION based social structure ie guilds.

So we have a 19th century missionary recording in the clearest terms that there was in existence in India a "wonderful institution" of guilds whose existence presented an obstacle to the acceptance of Christ, ie conversion.

To provide further confirmation of such a social structure, we find Sunderland writing : "The wealth of India was created by the Hindus vast and varied industries. Nearly every kind of manufacture or product known to the civilised world nearly every kind of creation of man's brain and hand, existing anywhere, and prized either for its utility or beauty had long, long been produced in India. India was a far greater industrial and manufacturing nation than any in Europe and or than any other in Asia, her textile goods – the fine products of her looms, in cotton wool linen and silk – were famous over the civilised world, so were the exquisite jewellery and her precious stones cut in every lovely form, so were her pottery, porcelains, ceramics of every kind, quality colour and beautiful shape, so were her fine works in metal, iron steel silver and gold. She had great architecture – equal in beauty to any in the world. She had great engineering works, She had great merchants, great businessman, great bankers and great financiers. Not only was she the greatest ship building nation, but she had commerce and trade by land and sea which extended to all known civilised countries. Such was the India which the British found when they came."

Within a hundred years of Anglican domination, millions of Hindus had died of famine and poverty and her economic infrastructure had been all but dismantled, converted into a resource extraction process of unyielding torture, horror and genocide. A nation which had never suffered famine saw its land being used instead by the British Anglicans to grow

Poppies for export to China in support of the British InterFaith activities with China, otherwise known as the Opium wars.

As computed by Brooks Adams in the 57 years from 1783 the Anglican pirates extorted or simply stole between 2.5 Billion and 5 Billion US Dollars out of India. Indeed records show that Robert Clive, the Anglican 1st Baron of Plassey sent 4 million dollars of plunder to Calcutta in one shipment alone, remarking "When I think of the marvellous riches of that country, and the comparatively small part which I took away, I am astonished at my own moderation".... One can't help again recalling Lord Deben's remarks about traditional British values.

The inherently fluid and naturally life-embracing wisdom of Varna, Jati, and Kul were deliberately and maliciously transmuted into clinically corrosive Caste and the cultural and religious deconstruction of the oldest living indigenous civilisation, the last remaining threat to global domination of the Church of Empire, began. In Lord Harries' amendment, it continues unabated, even today.

Caste, Varna, Jati & Kul

A s to 'Caste' – It first appears in mid-16th century Europe (in the general sense of 'race, breed'): from the Spanish and Portuguese casta 'lineage, race, breed', feminine of casto 'pure, unmixed', from Latin castus 'chaste'. Modern day Caste is defined as having three attributes – "hierarchical, endogamous & hereditary", and was the word describing the Portuguese and European social structure of Pope/Cardinals, Aristocracy, Merchants and 'Peasants'. There is no equivalent word or concept in the Hindu Scriptures and no identical structure either recorded or promoted in Hindu Scriptures. Caste is simply Portuguese for "Social Class"

As to 'Varna' - This is a Sanskrit word which means "type, order, colour or class." It more precisely means "variations/ variety, choice from a varied selection." As in Varmala – the Garland of choice used by a Hindu Princess at her Swayam-Var ("self choice") to declare to all her chosen suitor, the Var-nmala ie the alphabet – a garland of variations ie different sounds. Var like so many Sanskrit roots has found its way into English as in variation and variety.

In the context of the often deliberately and unknowingly misquoted core Hindu Scripture the Bhagavad Gita, Sri Krishna says "I have created 4 variations of person – the intellectual, the warrior, the trader and the labourer". There is no connection in the verse quoted with hereditary, no mention of hierarchy and no connection with endogamy. Indeed there are verses clearly denying the hereditary and hierarchical claims. Varna clearly does not mean a hereditary, hierarchical, endogamous social class structure, which is what the word "caste" means.

Sri Aurobindo, one of India's greatest Hindu saints recorded *"The spirit of ancient India was aristocratic; its thought and life moulded in the cast of a high and proud nobility, an extreme and lofty strenuousness. The very best in thought, the very best in action, the very best in character, the very best in literature and art, the very best in religion and all the world well lost if only this very best might be attained, such was the spirit of ancient India. The Brahmin who devoted himself to poverty and crushed down every desire in the wholehearted pursuit of knowledge and religious self-discipline; the Kshatriya who, hurling his life joyously into the shock of chivalrous battle, held life, wife, children, possessions, ease, happiness as mere dust in the balance compared with honour and the Kshatriya dharma, the preservation of self-respect, the protection of the weak, the noble fulfilment of princely duty; the Vaishya, who toiling all his life to amass riches, poured them out as*

46

soon as amassed in self-forgetting philanthropy, holding himself the mere steward and not the possessor of his wealth; the Shudra who gave himself up loyally to humble service, faithfully devoting his life to his dharma, however low, in preference to self-advancement and ambition; these were the social ideals of the age". This was the Hindu India the British discovered.

Historically, in India, just as in any nation anywhere in the world throughout history, sons and daughters followed in the footsteps of their fathers and a whole community was dedicated to single professions, preserving and refining the knowledge capital of a civilisation. But this is a universal social phenomena, whether it is the coal miners of America's Appalachian mountains or the cattle ranchers of Africa's nomadic tribes. There is also social injustice along these class/guild lines in many different countries not to mention the fault lines between Celtic and Rangers, Catholics and Protestants and so on.

But the Anglican British social engineers, by their own admission, were largely responsible for the deliberate corruption and attempted stratification of the fluid Varna system into a rigid Caste system in India, one which simultaneously destroyed the economic fabric of an ancient civilisation whilst destroying the cultural, spiritual and social heritage of a prosperous people.

There is ample evidence available for those impartial enough to seek it, confirming that the early Christian missionaries recognised that the social structure of India's millennia old Jati system was a marvel of organisation, occasionally even labelled as wonderful. At the time when religiously sanctioned Christian zealots, pirates and plunderers were engaged in the massacre of the indigenous Ganai peoples of Austrailia, Rev Joseph Roberts addressed a gathering of Missionaries in Madras on 4th January 1844. There are three elements noteworthy from his address (which is reproduced below)

The first is that the when he uses the word Caste – it is clear that he refers to Jati ie occupational Guild. Secondly he identifies the system of occupational guilds as "the great barrier in India betwixt Pagans and Christ", and finally he describes the system as "this wonderful institution of India". In a nutshell, in order to proselytise and convert, the Church missionaries needed to destroy the occupational guilds of India – so spoke a respected Reverend of the Christian establishment.

Noteworthy is the fact that whilst Brahmins were speaking of Varna (non hereditary, non hierarchical, non-endogamous aptitude-based divinity-inspired "spiritually egalitarian" and glorious humanity, Christian missionaries were hearing what suited their conversionary designs, they were hearing and preaching Caste. In the following, it is clear from the Reverends address that missionaries were delighted to overlook this inconvenient inaccuracy, either through lack of philosophical sophistication and spiritual experience or simply because it was strategically inconvenient to do so. In order to convert the infidel, they needed for Hindu society to be evil and for

Hindu society to be evil, they needed the Hindu religious teachings to be evil. The gold standard meritocracy-driven Varna concept as enshrined in Hindu scriptures and declared by Brahmin teachers and priests was transmuted into the leaden Christian construct of Caste, and exported back to Europe as the prime reason why domestic Christians needed to support the Church in its mission to civilise the heathen.

Little has changed.

II.

CASTE.

AN ADDRESS DELIVERED IN THE WESLEYAN MISSION CHAPEL,
MADRAS, AT THE MONTHLY MISSIONARY PRAYER-MEET-
ING, JANUARY 4TH, 1844, BEFORE THE MISSIONARIES OF
THE DIFFERENT CHURCHES, &c.

BY THE REV. JOSEPH ROBERTS,

CORRESPONDING MEMBER OF THE ROYAL ASIATIC SOCIETY OF GREAT
BRITAIN AND IRELAND, AUTHOR OF "ORIENTAL ILLUSTRA-
TIONS OF THE SACRED SCRIPTURES," &c., &c.

In consequence of *very strong opinions recently* put forth
in a Madras publication respecting Caste in the church, and
the sentiments still entertained by some Christians as to its
character and toleration; the determined adherence of numerous native members to this system, in the various duties
of life; and the solemn fact, that, next to the love of sin,
Caste is the great barrier in India betwixt the Pagans and
Christ; I have thought it advisable to call your attention to
this difficult and painful subject; and I do this the more
readily, because I possess the opinions of thirty-three Missionaries, collected by myself several years ago. For it appears to
me that such decided protests, against a measure fraught
with so much dissension and dereliction of duty, may be
profitable to those who are in doubts, and serve to confirm us
in our principles, which we believe to be in harmony with the
word of God.

To bring my plan more distinctly before your view, I
purpose, First, to consider the probable origin of Caste;
Secondly, its true spirit,—it is *religious* and civil; Thirdly,
its existence and character amongst the Native Christians; Fourthly, the reasons which induced me, in 1828, to
refer to my reverend brethren; and, Lastly, the extracts from
their several protests.

I. As to the origin of Caste, we are sometimes taken to
the fabulous stories and numerous conceits of priests and
others; declaring that the Brahmins came from the mouth
of the deity, to read, to teach, to pray; that the Cshetriyas
were from his arms, to fight, and govern; that the Vaisyas

were from the belly, to be employed in agriculture, and trade, and to furnish the necessaries of life; that the Sudras were from the feet, to labour, to serve, and travel; so that the divine sanction is here clearly asserted for the various divisions of men, leading the poor Hindus to conclude, that as they were *thus* created, so they must ever remain. We think, however, that this wonderful institution of India may be traced to a more probable source, merging in the wisdom and craft of man; as is seen in the account of its rise, in the Kings Solen, Searen, and Pandian, who were ably assisted by Katche-veerappen, the counsellor of the latter, to carry out its various ramifications amongst the people. At all events, there is something more rational in this relation than the former.

We are not, however, convinced that *all* the tyrannical notions ascribed to the human inventors of this classification of men can be received as correct; for we think it probable that, in the first instance, there was strong reference to the full, the due, and constant provision for all kinds of artizans and labourers; so that, in every emergency, there might be a supply of the required workmen, to meet the various wants of the realm. And we think it likely there would be another, though perhaps sequent, thought; namely, that, by fixing each person in his manual profession, there would be greater perfection secured in the several works of art; for the children, not being allowed to adopt any other calling, would naturally, from the first dawning of thought, associate themselves with their fathers' pursuits, and try to emulate each other in gaining the greatest reward. Just so the parents themselves would, on the due developement in their offspring of muscle and mind, take advantage of their aid, and in early life accustom them to use those implements or tools, which were never to be laid aside but by sickness or the grave. Nor was it forgotten to assign a fixed *locality* to those who followed a given occupation; so that, by sending to their quarters, some might always be found to supply the public need, and also secure greater peace amongst themselves. For if they had been allowed to reside there as rivals in rank, however slight the difference might be, still there would have been interminable broils, which never could have been removed or allayed except by the sovereign power. It is also probable, the originators of this arrangement would look forward to the *perpetuity* of each trade, so that they might feel assured that those most needful members of the state would never become extinct. For in such a rude age it is not to be supposed that men understood the relative importance of their different callings, and therefore they might be tempted to leave their own for others, which were more respectable, lucrative, or easy. Then, again, at that period, and in that reign, there could scarcely have been those known motives for competition, as when men are perfectly free; and when all have an equal opportunity for making the best of their skill and power, and have the certainty of being allowed to retain what they justly acquire; leading us also to another supposition, that it was not then perceived that any overplus in the workmen or the produce would compel men, by an unseen, unwritten law, to adopt other modes of living; and therefore the legislators determined to place each person in that caste and calling in which he and his posterity should ever remain.

Looking at the *present* numerical state of the several Castes, in their ratio to each other, we cannot help seeing an argument for the supposed *original* number needed for every trade; because, in the *first* aggregates, reference would be made to the various duties of life, and to the *required* supplies. For it is absurd to suppose there would be the same proportion of men assigned to those callings where few hands were needed, as to such where the demand was the greatest: for instance, the rulers would not in the beginning appoint as many to be barbers, as cultivators; or potters, as carpenters and masons. Hence we see, at this distant period, the quota bears an exact relation to what we believe to have been the case in ancient times, as those occupations least in request would have the fewest workmen: so they show at this date how nature has maintained the original order.

But though we may give credit to the early sovereigns and others, for having had a reference to the mechanical and agricultural wants of the kingdom, in their arrangement of Castes and professions, yet we cannot persuade ourselves that men of such sagacity would not also perceive, that, in the rival combinations and claims, materials would be formed for a more easy governing of the whole, as they would keep each other in abeyance, and thus be the willing instruments of the monarch's will. We may rely upon it, the subjugation of one caste to another was looked upon as congenial to the public peace; for the question was not in that day, whether the pacific principle should be founded upon equal civil and religious privileges, but on the fictitious, the unjust claims of family and birth; apart from all those reasons which alone can entitle men in civilized and Christian lands to the preeminence and distinctions which confer station, wealth, and fame.   The oriental rulers resolved, if possible, to keep their subjects, like statues from the chisel of the sculptor, fixed in their own positions; they made fetters for the body, mind, and spirit, showing they preferred the submission of the slave to the obedience of the free; and in this way have they crippled the genius of the people, carving and shaping it to the directions and dimensions of known laws; so that the beautiful and useful productions which spring from the minds of free men, never adorn and bless these lands.

The sciences, the learning, the professions, the callings, the implements, and instruments of antiquity, are deemed all that men require, producing that fixedness of intellect so common amongst the Hindus, making it like something from a mould, or as wax from the seal, retaining faithfully its first impression.

The penultimate paragraph is pure conjecture and the last paragraphs graphically demonstrate the theocrats inability to appreciate the subtlety of the "wonderful" system they had discovered and in the words that followed, one can see the asset stripping minds superimposition at work, even in 1844. By the time the Criminal Tribes Act was completed in 1871, the above teachings had been imparted in the Colonial colleges of England, the institutions which specialised in preparing the Lord Lundy's of Victorian England to "Lord over the dark skinned heathen" and the transformation of the understanding of Jati had been successfully morphed into the horror of

"India's Hindu Caste system". This is the lie that is still spouted with such confidence in many corners of decaying Colonialism even today, and this is the untruth which was peddled in the House of Lords, on 4th March 2013.

Does social injustice that falls along class lines exist in India? Of course, as it does in Great Britain and in the US, where they have a prison population of 85% black men, yet no one places this problem at the feet of Christianity, even though a clear connection can be made to certain verses in the Bible, slavery and even current day race relations in many countries. The Rockefellers and Lords of London are not dining with the janitors of London, while the rich get richer and the poor get poorer. Unlike the case of India and Hindus, no one ascribes this social injustice to a religion. The Lords are not troubled by the horrific racism statistics propelling America's

#BlackLivesMatter initiative and yet the mission of elevating the British Hindus out of their backward ways, like a lodestone drawing iron filings, perennially draws all of their attention – and we are asked to believe that it has nothing to do with conversion.

"No aspect of Indian society is as poorly understood as its social organization. The caste system, as described in Indian textbooks, is a creation of the anthropologists and sociologists of the nineteenth century who were then studying the bewildering complexity of Indian society. The informants of these social scientists used the theories of the archaic Dharma Sastras to fit the communities in a

four-varna model. Although such classification was wrong, it has been used by generations of Indologists and filtering into popular books it has, by endless repetition, received a certain validity and authority. In an example of reality being fashioned in the image of a simulacrum, many Indians have started believing in the enduring truth of the classification (Subash Kak,1994)"

Caste as a concept, practice and social cancer is purely and exclusively a European Christian Colonial creation, and has no roots nor support in any Hindu ideology. The Church of England is responsible for every hateful act resulting from their perpetuation of the "bespoke Indian Caste" concept and it is the Church that must now be held accountable.

The Victims and Casualties of the Lord Harries Amendment

A nd what of the casualties of this ill-conceived, malicious piece of legislative mischief, which is deliberately disruptive of interfaith harmony and community cohesiveness?

It has been established from statutory records, (Appendix A) that the Church of England fully supported Lord Harries' faithless, supremacist expedition, despite the window dressing of shallow disingenuous murmurs of disapproval. It would also appear that Lord Harries was willing to abuse and pervert the dignity of even the House of Lords, an institution which should be a force for security, stability and service to British citizens of all religious and non-religious traditions, in the furtherance of the conversionary agenda of the Church of England. That Lambeth Palace was selfishly pursuing its own spiritually bankrupt agenda in trying to resurrect its colonial policy of "divide and rule", is now very difficult to refute and cannot be swept under the carpet.

Like all fraudulent scams and schemes, a time comes when such duplicity is revealed and placed upon display for all to see and that too is fast approaching. This manipulation of the legislative process, destructive of community cohesion, if sanctioned, supported and specifically approved of by Lambeth Palace, will have immeasurable consequences. The impact of this action on British interfaith dialogue is at present, like thunder rumbling in the distance, but fast approaching. British Hindus and members of other Dharmic traditions are asking the question - "On what basis should the Dharmic communities trust any member of the Anglican clergy, ever again?" Are we moving towards the end of all authentic Anglican-Hindu InterFaith dialogue?

The assertion that the Church of England acted in bad faith, knowingly and deliberately for its own sectarian, anti-Hindu evangelical objectives, has been established with a far greater degree of evidence than the foundational "truth claims" upon which even its own core evangelical mission is constructed. Most pertinently the fact of the Church's betrayal of a sacred national trust is also established with far greater evidence than that presented in support of this act of religious persecution, couched as a legislative clause, allegedly in protection of Equality and human rights.

The House of Lords will not recover any shred of its already weather-beaten and tarnished reputation until relief has been provided for the Hinduodic hate crime perpetrated upon British Hindus by the Upper Chamber. The fact that such discriminatory, prejudiced and cynical manipulation was concealed and presented as "Equality legislation", legislation designed to protect the vulnerable from the powerful, should give grave concern for all legislators as to the real ability of the Upper Chamber to protect the needs of the most vulnerable, least culpable members of British society. There are Parliamentary processes and Government bodies such as the GEO and the EHRC whose very purpose, whose "raison d'etre", is to prevent a skilful bigoted orator from manipulating emotions whilst at the same time inflicting human rights abuses

– this whole Caste issue is a sad reflection upon all of these bodies and has created a question mark over their real world "suitability for purpose".

It should be clear to any impartial legislator that this law <u>denies</u> every British Hindu the right to be treated as equal to any other British Hindu, and in enshrining in law the false premise of the "Indic Caste system" further demotes from a position of equality with all other British communities, all of the Dharmic communities. It creates the very inequality which equalities legislation is intended to challenge. It is the only piece of legislation to have been passed which enshrines a presumption of inequality and it was introduced by a representative of the "by law established" dominant religious institution of the United Kingdom.

What is starkly unavoidable and quite extraordinary is that from all of the political parties, Government departments, Parliamentary APPG's, Equality NGO's, Human Rights Champions and Legal eagles, Ministers and Peers, the ONLY body which agreed to inspect the data and evidence and to consider the impact in an impartial manner, was the Government headed by PM David Cameron, surviving the unrelenting pressure of even a coalition Government partner.

In time to come, this pivotal insistence on due process, community consultation and scrutiny by the Conservative Government will be noted with deep gratitude by all Hindus in all nations and by true proponents of religious freedoms. History will record that whilst Labour leader Hon Jeremy Corbyn was standing by his dishonourable and wholly inflated claim that there were "1 million Dalits in the UK" (as opposed to the census record of circa 15,000), the integrity and reputation of Parliamentary process was itself protected by only Prime Minister David Cameron and his Conservative party.

All others danced blindly, intoxicated by the emotionally manipulative tune so skilfully played by the Pied Piper of Pentregarth and we all need to give serious consideration upon how they permitted themselves and their prejudices to be so easily manipulated. Hon Lord Popat, Hon Alok Sharma

MP, Hon Bob Blackman MP, Hon Paul Uppal MP are to be acknowledged for adhering to the principle of scrutiny of the actual evidence, as opposed to yielding to the "religious persecution" based smear campaign being wielded by the supporters of this amendment.

The, clearly unwholesome, presence of 26 Bishops in the Upper Chamber is a theocratic pothole on the British "roadmap" and journey towards genuine interfaith harmony, especially at the very dawn of a post theocratic, post colonial British community, Europe and world. As many legal experts have repeated in the Houses of Parliament and elsewhere, this most intransigent Church of Empire cannot be relied upon to deliver justice and protection of Human rights to its own members, at this time it clearly can no longer be entrusted with the most delicate and sensitive work of our time, Inter-Faith engagement either.

Recognition, Remorse, Reparation and Reconciliation

On the basis of the evidence above, as well as innumerable other records of impeccable and unimpeachable provenance, it is clear that the suffering of Hindus at the hands of Anglicans is one of recent history's unreported "crimes against humanity" including genocide and that there are millions of Hindus who have been devastated by the atrocities inflicted upon them, and as a result of which they are still struggling every day. We look forward to hearing from the Archbishop of Canterbury, the Rt. Honourable Justin Welby, his proposals with regard to justice and reparation for the Hindu, whether Dalit or Non Dalit, British or Indian for past hate crimes and anticipated hate crimes, perpetrated by his Institution or with its blessings and "Divine" sanction, encouragement and support.

Conclusions

The British Hindu community asked the protectors of Equality "Did no one in the Upper Chamber even think to check the context, the data and the possible motives before embarking on this 21st Century Witch Hunt?" Or even worse can no religious minority now rely on the Upper Chamber or British Human Rights bodies for protection from the religious persecution being so skilfully perpetrated by the majority aggressively evangelical religion? The House of Lords needs to justify its competence, perhaps its very existence, once again, thanks to Lord Harries of Pentregarth. It is respectfully suggested, that only once it has been purged of those who act with blatantly sectarian, wholly non-secular and supremacist motives, can it rightfully be a voice for the good of all British citizens, especially the minority Dharmic, non-aggressive, non- conversionary British Jains, Sikhs and Hindus.

The 18th century Anglican mission of "One Church to rule them all and One Church to find them, one church to bring them all and in the darkness bind them.." seems less incredible now than it did before the 4th March 2013.

It is our hope that once all see the above design laid out before them, the gentle deeply philosophical and entirely peaceful depths of the Dharmic community's presence will be also increasingly accepted and appreciated again, as is the Dharmic vision of harmonious community co-existence. The insane pursuit of "Unity in conformity", the mainstay of this Anglican Institution, will have been seen to again have generated friction and dischord, and the ancient Dharmic principle of "Unity in Diversity" will again come to the fore, bringing tranquillity and harmony with it.

And what of the Caste concept itself? Once the psychological virus, which is the caste concept, has been removed, dissolved from humanity's consciousness, the Dharmic traditions, free of this cancerous, wholly Colonialist Anglican ideology, will again be able to contribute their 5,000- year-old holistic, inclusive, respectful vision of tranquil co-existence. Enshrining the concept of Caste in law, under the guise of equality legislation is a retrograde step which will enforce its resurrection here in the UK of the 21st Century. A fuller explanation of the science, social and material behind Jati, Varna and Kul and Gotra, will be presented in the full British Board of Dharmic Scholars (BBDS) Report on the Caste Legislation, of which this forms a part and which will be published shortly.

It should now be clear that by entrenching a falsified and fabricated, Christian concept of Caste into Law, the Church of England sought to protect its centuries old anti-Hindu negative-branding project. The "divide and rule" policy being so skilfully executed to separate and maintain distance between Dharmic communities along the lines of Caste required the concept of Caste to be enshrined in law. This would allow Christian Clergy the world over to leverage the concept as a platform from which to denigrate the oldest most tranquil spiritual tradition in the world, thereby facilitating "easy conversionary pickings" year after year, generation after generation.

We are at a juncture in British Indian history where the past atrocities instigated and often inflicted by this Institution, have now been brought centre stage. Very soon they will be appearing on every negotiating table and will become the subject of every post Brexit trade dialogue or political engagement. The British Government, obliged and desirous of acting on behalf of all of the British people will falter and stumble each time the issue of the Churches sponsored and supported past atrocities are revealed, not just in the Indian context but in the global context. It is clear that without the help and active support of the British Hindu community, the past cannot be reconciled and a path towards a mutually Indo British respectful future, with both nations benefiting will not so easily be laid.

It's also self-evident that only in a world where Dharmic ideals are providing guidance (as was the case in pre-Abrahamic days) can intercultural harmony exist. We must recognise the Dharmic principles which teach that

- none are deemed sinners at birth, nor criminal at birth

- none can claim exclusive entry to higher realms of consciousness,

- no theocracy is required for humanity to exist according to our naturally endowed higher qualities and aspirations,

- Divinity can be found in the deepest heart of all people simply by sustained tranquil introspection,

- thus all are truly equal in the eyes of Divinity.

Consider a possibly extreme, light hearted example. Even if one think's that the "Hare Krishna's" are a little "dynamic" in their devotion, it is certain that if all humanity were "Hare Krishna's", there would be food for all, more dancing and singing and no religious warfare. The same applies to all members of the Dharmic family of spiritual traditions. The record (as opposed to the marketing literature) of the Abrahamic traditions of enforcing with violence, their exclusivist, aggressive insistence on uniformity and submission over 2,000 years, rests in stark contrast and is also plain to see.

It has not escaped our attention that this issue has been the favoured "stomping ground" of vast hordes of "academics" and politicians, many of whom have made lifelong careers by ensuring that this long standing wound in the psyche and the body of the former colony is not permitted to heal, and by diligently avoiding any number of solutions. Many "academics" and Anglican Bishops have beaten their breasts with indignation, fueled with cheap moral indignation and ever present self righteousness and yet how many have accomodated the historical facts presented by an insignificant and unpolished community organisation such as the NCHT(UK)? These academicks, these Bishops and these scholars MUST be asked this question ... where did all that "public purse supported" research funding go?

They must also be asked, that if the obvious solution is to reverse the harm done by the Anglican colonial power and to re-unite the Dharmic family, why is it that every solution presented by them after all of their lifetimes of study, revolves around the denigration and vilification of the Dharmic religions and the conversion of their communities from their "false religion" to Christianity?

Pseudo academics play many games, most pernicious of which involves the maintenance of endless public funded "academicking" ie mimicking real academic effort and this activity can be best seen in the endless circles of peer reviewed self referential, generally unintelligible, nonsense which emerges. A recent academick escapade, at the taxpayers expense, sought to define Caste and concluded that an "elastic definition" was necessary, overlooking the fact that no definition by definition can be elastic, since in being elastic it ceases to define. Obvious to any A level student and yet this was the output of the EHRC, and its preferred vastly experienced academicks, all at the public expense.

Recalling the words of the ancient Hindu Mundaka Upanishad, and the Indian national motto, 'Satyam Eva Jayate – truth/reality alone triumphs', recalling also St Augustine's pronouncement "truth does not need to be defended, it is a lion and merely needs to be released", we present our understanding of the truth of the Bishop Lord Harries "Caste Amendment".

We shall be encouraging all British Hindus, Sikhs and Jains to give the deepest reflection as to whether there is benefit in adopting a policy of avoiding Anglican Clergy altogether. If it is agreed that in the opinion of the Dharmic Organisations who will be sent a copy of this note, that the Church of England has acted in bad faith and aggressively towards British Hindus, Sikhs and Jains, we may have no choice

but to explore all avenues to ensure the protection and wellbeing of our Dharmic community against the aggression of the professional Clergy of the Church of England, whilst welcoming closer interaction with grass roots Anglicans and Christians, especially those no longer infected with supremacist conversionary predatorial predilections.

The permanent solution to eradicating any Caste discrimination is to erase the Colonial concept of Caste from Consciousness altogether and clearly not to preserve and sustain it, by enshrining it in Law.

The Global Hindu community can then turn its attention to recognising and acknowledging fully the incomprehensible suffering of the "Dalit" community and their ancestors at the hands of the Anglican Colonialists, to helping their communities back to health and prosperity as Hindu brothers and sisters, from a position of respect and fraternity, fully equal members of the Dharmic family. This without, it must be noted, the help, guidance, or advice from any third person wishing to carry the "White man's burden" thank you very much.

"The Government's commitment to tackling hate crime is underpinned by some of the strongest legislation in the world, which protects communities from hostility, violence and bigotry. This includes specific offences for racially and religiously aggravated activity and offences of the stirring up of hatred on the grounds of race, religion and sexual orientation. It is imperative that those laws are rigorously enforced". Rt Hon Amber Judd, Home Secretary"

The British Hindu community recognises that many who are innocent of Hindu-odium, merely trusting of the Anglican Bishops and of the members of the Upper Chamber, will have come under the sway of a passionate but unevidenced and prejudicial arguments and we look forward to working with them to undo the harm which has been done to the British Dharmic community. They have the opportunity to approach us which we would welcome, and to offer their support in reversing the effects of this act of malice and we look forward to hearing from them. Together we will find means to repair the harm and as the "good book" says by their works shall ye know them.

In conclusion we would like to thank Lord Harries for giving us an opportunity to draw the attention of the wider British public to the tragic and cynical machinations of the Church of England, past and present, and forcing upon us the necessity, however misguided and unintended, to share the truth behind the creation of "Dalits" and "Caste" as well as being able to draw a contrast between the violent history of the Church of England and the Anglicans who acted in accordance with its teachings, and the most ancient and longstanding of Dharmic values, with our fellow British citizens.

An Appeal to "Dalits"

The Church of Empire drove your ancestors from their homes and trades, put them in chains and destroyed your spirit, simply because your ancestors resisted the tyrannical British Colonial Laws. The Colonial Anglicans then declared your whole community as "criminals by birth" … and for 200 years they have been blaming your own family members, brother and sister Hindus Sikhs and Jains, the "non-Dalits", for your plight.

Please reflect upon the motives of those who have done this to us and those who have benefitted from sustaining and inflaming this family rift. Irrespective of colour or religion, whether we see them as our own or as others, those who divided us for political gain or favour, they are the source of unimaginable suffering, within our family. Those who seek to exploit this wound even today, whether it is for reasons of conversion, academic patronage, political advancement or personal prominence, now know the real cause of the Dalit suffering and their conscience must ask "Who benefits from prolonging this rift and who is truly going to continue to suffer?" Knowing now the truth of the source of Dalit suffering, we each need to re-assess our loyalties and choose our "camp" – the colonial evangelicals or our ancestral brothers and sisters, all of whom were victims of the Anglican Jihad.

We are led to believe that the Anglican white supremacists who were responsible of enslaving Indian and other non-white nations and cultures, suddenly disappeared in 1947, being replaced by a benevolent, paternal, welcoming Clergy and "fairy godmother" establishment. The process of this legislation, its creation and guidance through Parliament, its approval by the EHRC and the Governments Equality Office, the existence of this word Caste in legislation at this very time, requires this assumption to be scrutinised as a matter of urgency, if multicultural interfaith harmony and social integration is to be achieved.

An Appeal to Hindus, Sikhs & Jains – British and Non British, White and non-white.

The Author and associated Hindu Scholars express their deepest gratitude and acknowledges their debt to the Dharmic wise ones in our families and the intellectuals, teachers, gurus and priests of all Jatis, Kul and Biradri's whether Kshatriya, Vaishya or Shudra, whether, Hindu, Sikh, Buddhist or Jain, the true Brahmins of India, for their sacrifices and determination to ensure that the Dharmic knowledge of our ancestors should not die – humanity is indebted to you and all will see this soon. We declare upon the strength of the evidence provided that your ancestors were not guilty of "caste discrimination" and that our scriptures and sages have always challenged ignorance and prejudice at every turn.

For the younger British Hindus who have recently become concerned that their ancestors were "casteist" we state with certainty that they were not. You are descendants and inheritors of the last great life affirming, free thinking civilisation extant and your ancestors were NOT CASTE PREJUDICED. Many of our contemporaries in India were infected, and continue to be infected with this Colonial legacy, this mental virus and we must help them to recover from it with all speed. Shed your burden of guilt, it is founded upon baseless accusations made by invaders and pirates, the worst the world has ever seen, of whom Tagore said "the sun never sets upon their Empire because not even God can trust the British in the Dark". You are free to stand tall and give voice to the vision of your ancestors.

Resume your caste free friendships and seek especially to give respect to our Dalit brothers and sisters, they have suffered as much as all of us at the hands of these Anglican Colonialists, even if in different ways, and in many ways their physical suffering was and continues to be at a level at least matching the evils inflicted upon the Aboriginals in Australia, the Native and African slaves in the Americas. It is time for them to come home, welcome them.

An Appeal to British Christians

Please study and scrutinise the sources mentioned above and in the bibliography and realise that the perpetrators of these Colonial "crimes against humanity" inflicted these policies of "divide and rule" FIRST upon the natives of these very islands, the British Isles. Reflect upon the manner in which the Dalits were created and then reflect upon the attitude towards the English peasantry, the Irish, the Scots and the Celts. Recall that the agents of this Church of Empire came back to this country and lied about the cultures and civilisations which they had encountered in the lands of "Johnny Foreigner".

Whilst erasing indigenous societies and populations on distant continents, they lied at home about the truly glorious and diverse history of a global humanity and they concealed and manipulated accounts of their own guilt and perverse violence. Your children are already exploring the wider world and the richness of eastern cultures and history, now even from their very phones, with eyes open to time and space, they are seeing the falsehood and fear that the Church of Empire has built its empire upon – go find out for yourself if what the Church fathers and Bishops have been telling your children and yourselves is true. The reason pews and Anglican Churches are empty is because your descendants are freeing themselves of fear and falsehood, the critical lies which the Church of Empire wielded to maintain its grip on its enslaved population, and which are the sands upon which this Institution stands today. The glaring dischord between the Gospel of Christ and the Church of Empire can no longer be ignored if there is to be any tranquillity between British faiths, traditions and religions - it is still very much present and lies at the heart of InterFaith dialogue in our 21st Century Britain.

Please muster extraordinary courage and just consider the possibility that the strategy which brands an innocent brown Hindu in rural India as a member of the "Criminal by Birth Tribe" is the same doctrine which has branded humans "Sinners by Birth" by the same Institution for centuries.

If you are repelled by the concept of whole tribes being "Criminal by Birth" why do you accept that your own children are "Sinners by Birth"? Your children and our children are increasingly free again and they will grow into full complete human beings, free from the "heart stifling" guilt of being "Criminals/Sinners by birth". They are also free from the second mental virus, the mind-numbing reason-crippling disempowering doctrine of blind loyalty to a small group of sad, grey unstable and unhappy men, otherwise known as "the Church".

Your children are already becoming what Christ envisioned when he declared "greater things than these shall ye do" and it will be, simply because of their freedom from the mental slavery of the Church of Empire. Once they are completely free of these two psychological viruses, their contribution to the world will be earth shaking, healing and liberating and the ripples of its arrival are already visible to those who care to look.

An Appeal to British "Pagans", the Original Dharmic Community of the UK

The same institution which inflicted horrors dredged up from the depths of hell and rained them down upon your mothers and sisters in its depravity, which then denigrated your worship of Mother Nature and the Earth for a millennia of years and which, gave unofficial sanction to the hate filled "WitchFinder General", did the same to all who respected the very earth which gives us life and sustenance, the world over. When they had finished here in these British Isles, they carried their hate filled pogroms of extermination of all indigenous knowledge systems, the wisdom that comes to gentle tranquil minded people naturally, and violently replaced it with blind destructive and divisive, supremacist belief. They came to India and, the Jewel in the Crown and flooded the country with the same rivers of pain and suffering, only 100,000 times over.

The Dharmic community declares its sympathy for your suffering and declares that your ancient holistic traditions resonate with ours. We have not only a shared vision of the Earth as Mother, of Humanity as inherently Divine by birth, but also a shared pain received at the violent hands of the same institution, the Church of Empire.

An Appeal to
Anglican Clergy

S tudy the history of your ancestors and your institution, the above is becoming common knowledge throughout the world, particularly in the coming days weeks and months and years, simply because we are in the time when no hate-filled misdeeds can remain secret.

Your institutions' abuse spanning cultures and continents, encompassing vulnerable far off civilisations to vulnerable British children in London itself, is plain to see for all and becoming impossible to conceal or deny. Your corporation has grown fat by feeding on the life energy of the British people of all traditions and of "foreigners" for millennia, by instilling fear and hatred, by dividing and ruling as opposed to uniting and serving. Its history of abuse and exploitation of the English and the non-English, calls to you for justice with flowing tears, calling from the mouths of every soul this institution has tormented in this country and around the world. There is a limit to how much suffering any corporation can inflict upon humanity and a day of reckoning fast approaches.

Are you, as persons on a declared quest for divinity loyal to the victims, the people, the children of this Earth or to this institution whose very name is globally synonymous with exploitation in the name of Divinity?

We urge you to make that choice today, remembering that the consequences of taking the name of Divinity in vain, especially for the gratification of personal ambition or salacious appetites, at the expense of the innocent and vulnerable, is the greatest of all sins.

Message to Chair, Equalities and Human Rights Commission (EHRC)

The EHRC supported and participated in the perpetration of a Hate Crime against the British Hindu Sikh and Jain communities. When the truth of their actions was brought to the attention of the EHRC team and Project Leader, in multiple correspondences and whilst interacting with the InterFaith Network, the complaints were shrugged off as meaningless and of no consequence. The EHRC "Caste legislation" project was biased, prejudiced and contemptuous of the British Dharmic Community from the very outset, with even the EHRC's own website declaring the desired outcome and the religious and philosophical orientations long before the project was even commenced. The British Dharmic Community were assumed guilty, without evidence or trial and the EHRC gave official sanction to this act of Religious Hatred. The Governments Hate Crime Plan states:-

There are three categories of hate crime in legislation:

- *incitement to hatred offences on the grounds of race, religion or sexual orientation;*

- *specific racially and religiously motivated criminal offences (such as common assault); and*

- *provisions for enhanced sentencing where a crime is motivated by race, religion,*

The Governments published statement clarifies that *"Hate crimes are pernicious; they send the message that some people deserve to be targeted solely because of who they are or <u>who they are believed to be</u>."*

Your organisation pandered to the desire of Lord Harries and his "anti-Hindu" coterie in proliferating without evidence that CASTE was a reality for British Hindus, when there is more than ample evidence that the community groups are merely geographical, ancestrally occupational, or religious denominations. Your organisation supported fully the attempts to misrepresent these groupings as a "caste system" an attribute of a barbaric community and therefore worthy of vilification and denigration.

Your organisation gave official sanction and fully participated in "incitement to hatred offences on the grounds of race, <u>religion</u> or sexual orientation". Therefore the British Dharmic community has NO confidence in the EHRC as the custodian and guardian of our human rights and equality legislation. Once again we remind you that this is an injustice of the greatest magnitude and one which cannot disappear. Like all hate crimes the ripples of such a hate inspired act will ripple ever outwards and it will persist in consciousness until justice and reparations have been made. Since all other communication has been dismissed, perhaps this report could be assumed to be a formal complaint, prior to our proceeding with a request for a full Judicial Review.

Any crime that is motivated by hostility on the grounds of race, religion, sexual orientation, disability or transgender identity can be classed as a hate crime.

The Colonialists Mantra
"Divide & Rule"

1. Identify an area of human activity
2. Note a distribution of success
3. Identify winners and losers
4. Claim that the losers are losing only because they are oppressed by the winners.
5. Claim allegiance with the losers
6. Feel secure in your comprehensive explanation of the world
7. Revel in your moral superiority
8. Target your resentment towards your newly discovered enemies
9. Repeat. Forever. Everywhere.

- Dr. Jordan B. Peterson

Message to Archbishop Justin Welby, Lambeth Palace

With regard to this Christian supremacist and colonialist "Caste legislation", you have an opportunity to make some small atonement to help right an injustice which has caused pain and suffering to millions, for almost 300 years. Your Institution is directly responsible and is soon to be held accountable on the global stage, for the decades of torture and murder which transformed the courageous Hindu and Sikh tribes who challenged the criminal Anglican expansion into India, in to the long suffering people today known as the Dalits.

Your Institution provided the moral and religious approval which led to the inflicting upon them, of unbearable levels of contempt, poverty and denigration, filling them with justifiable rage permeating generations. We submit that your Institution then groomed, radicalised and converted their own vulnerable and dependent children, and further directed this rage towards their own indigenous culture, history, civilisation and finally at their own Hindu brothers and sisters. Lord Harries' actions are entirely consistent with the white supremacist colonialist tradition and history of your institution and are evidence of a continuation of the tired old religiously predatorial colonialist policies.

THE CLEMENCY OF CANNING.

Governor-General. "WELL, THEN, THEY SHANT BLOW HIM FROM NASTY GUNS; BUT HE MUST PROMISE TO BE A GOOD LITTLE SEPOY."

We overlooked the self- delusional remarks made by your predecessor in 2007 when he remarked that the "British experiment in India was an example of caring colonialism" but your institutions' sustained attack upon Hindus must cease. Muslims in their Mosques are not having meetings about the terrible "Hindu Caste" system, neither are the Jewish, Zoroastrian, Pagan, Mormon community, why is Lambeth Palace stoking the fires of intra – community friction? Dame Louise Casey's report highlights the failure of InterFaith in this country and if the interference and deliberate denigration of the British Hindu community is anything to judge by, it's perfectly possible that the failure of InterFaith in this country is by design and not by lack of effort nor lack of public funding. As the prime custodian and directional force behind the current InterFaith vision, responsibility for such failure must be placed at the gates of Lambeth Palace and the question of conflict of interest is now a worthy question. Is it possible that the failure of InterFaith can be to the advantage of the Church established by Law? As CEO of this corporation, on the strength of all of the evidence presented and much more yet to be presented, the British Hindus call upon you to respond and to account for these acts, for these centuries of Hate Crimes against vulnerable children, peoples and indigenous cultures.

Message to Lord Harries, our "Pied Piper of Pentregarth"

I am not an academic in the conventional sense of the word but my strongest credentials are that I was brought up in the stolid gritty East Midlands of the 60's, with the firmly Dharmic, Hindu and English tradition of resisting bullying and prejudice coupled, with the Midlanders finely tuned "flannel" detector. I write as a British citizen, living and revelling in being such in this country at this challenging time. I write in service not of those who live in the rarefied atmospheres of Palaces (either educational, political or religious) but in the service of those British citizens struggling to make sense of a world in flux and desperate to make friends and build diverse harmonious communities, citizens like myself.

I write as a person, born to Hindu parents, in a Brahmin "Kul" (lineage), a Kshatriya's (Warrior) "Varna" (aptitude/ human variety), within the Pandit "Jati" (Guild), with Rishi Gotra's as my genetic lineages, working as a "Vaishya" Businessman "Jati" (Guild), a Brahmin teacher "Jati" (occupation) and in the garden under the guidance of my dear wife at weekends, as a Shudra (manual worker). I am a member of the Punjabi Doaba, Anglican schooled, British-Indian-NRI-Delhiite-Nottingham Forest supporting, Vegetarian-Samosa loving Biradri's (brotherhoods/communities) many of which I share with my Sikh, Jain Gujarati, Muslim and Christian friends and families. And I am at ease with all of the diverse flavours of my identity, each bringing unimaginable gifts and challenges in delightfully unequal measure and I have never discriminated against any other human being.

Having expended so much time and effort, having disbursed public and government funds in their millions in trying to shoehorn me into a legal box consistent with your seemingly diabolical design, please consult with your "lead expert" Dr Meena Dhanda, your discriminatory, pseudo experts at NIESR, the Equalities and Human Rights Commission and the Government Equalities Office, and the Doyens of the Labour and Liberal Democrat parties, and do send me a legally sound certificate enlightening me as to what my "Caste" is? I look forward to appearing in front of Justices one day to hear them attempt to define me.

I could provide you with the similarly diverse and colourful profiles of my British parents and British children if it would help but you would need to determine the caste of a Punjabi born retired Bus-driver who is a teacher of the Vedas, a volunteer who has built both Gurudwaras and Temples and is a scholar of the Granth Sahib as well as Punjabi poetry, who writes in Urdu as fluently as he does in Punjabi, Hindu and English, not to mention a mother who loves the Punjabi Sikh Sukhmani Saahb as much as she does the Hindu Chandi Paath. I respectfully deny you the right to put us in your Evangelists "legislation by vilification" created, discrimination driven, colonialists box.

"Any crime that is motivated by hostility on the grounds of race, religion, sexual orientation, disability or transgender identity can be classed as a hate crime." Rt Honourable Home Secretary Amber Rudd MP

To dispel any remaining shred of doubt, This "criminal by birth" approach to enshrining Caste into Law, seeks to make prejudice and hatred of Hindus, Sikhs & Jains, the law of the land.

It is in itself, by all definitions, a Hate Crime.

To assume that all persons who have a surname associated with an ancestral profession, are potentially guilty of being "caste supremacist" is itself an act of prejudice.

To include into law a colonial missionary trope is akin to accepting into law, equally reprehensible tropes such as the "blood libel" against the Jewish people, the "Rapist" libel against Americas Blacks, the "born criminal" libel against Europe's Romany community.

Notable is the coincidence that all of these tropes have the same ethnic and religious source.

We conclude as follows with the daily Hindu prayer "Aum Sarve Bhavantu Sukinah" from the ancient Brihadaaranyaka Upanishad 1.4.14, with a slight modification of our own:--

Aum, May All become Happy, May all be Free from Illness, May All See what is Auspicious, May no one suffer, Aum Tranquility, Tranquility, Tranquility, Aum , And may all such wholly hateful attempts to enshrine prejudice and discrimination into Law be repealed and never again see the light of day

And may Caste Consciousness be erased in its entirety.

Pt Satish K Sharma

@dharmarising

www.satishksharma.com

www.castebomb.com

Bibliography

It is commonplace to present a bibliography to make the appearance of a pseudo academic work complete and we too have one to offer, but one with slight modification. The sources we have referred to in our work are listed below but we choose not to fuel lazy pseudo academicking by providing page/para details in all cases. This issue has consumed 3 years of British Dharmic volunteer time, not to mention vast amounts of public funding. It has further created great suffering amongst the global Dharmic community, especially in India where the harmful after effects of Anglican "divide and rule" radicalisation continue to destroy otherwise harmonious communities and lives to this day. The Caste Conspiracy has the potential to cause possibly terminal harm to global Inter Faith integration and community cohesion. The matter warrants the highest level of attention from the academic and the political community and we would advise ALL to read ALL of the material presented below to become fully informed and genuinely educated in this matter. Thank you.

1. http://www.publications.parliament.uk/pa/
    ld201213/ldhansrd/text/130304-0001.htm

2. http://nchtuk.org/index.php/component/content/
    article/8-news/latest-news/346-hindu-christian-
    under- scrutiny

3. https://www.gov.uk/government/publications/
    hate-crime-action-plan-2016

4. http://www.mycasteishindu.org/

5. https://en.wikipedia.org/wiki/Criminal_Tribes_Act

6. https://hansard.digiminster.com/Lords/2016-07-11/
    debates/16071120000176/Caste- BasedDiscrimination#
    contribution-16071125000011

7. https://www.gov.uk/government/publications/
    hate-crime-action-plan-2016

8. https://en.wikipedia.org/wiki/Hinduism_in_the_
    United_Kingdom

9. http://timesofindia.indiatimes.com/world/uk/
    Church-of-England-head-lauds-British- Raj/
    articleshow/2569688.cms

10. creative.sulekha.com/review-of-rakesh-bahadur-s-
    equality-and-inclusion-by-dr-shrinivas- tilak_542824_
    blog

11. India in Bondage, Dr J T Sunderland (1929)

12. http://www.un.org/esa/socdev/unpfii/documents/ DRIPS_en.pdf

13. Dishonoured by History: "Criminal Tribes" and British Colonial Policy, Meena Radhakrishna

14. The Making of a Colonial Stereotype – The Criminal Tribes and Castes of India by Sanjay Nigam

15. Racism without the Racists – Eduardo Bonilla-Silva (2nd edition 2006)

16. The British Dominion & Conquest of India, Sir Penderel Moon (1989)

17. The Case for India , Will Durrant

18. *Transactions of the New York State Agricultural Society*, Vol 19, 1859, p. 230

19. "Inglorious Empire - What the British Did to India" Dr Shashi Tharoor

JUSTICE.

"White and Black…"

Appendices

Letter from Mike Purton (1st March 2017)

(A former BBC television producer and writer on spiritual matters)

EQUALITY ACT 2010 AMENDMENT

I have been shocked by your assessment of the Lord Harries amendment and your interpretation of the real intentions behind it. While accepting your outline of the events leading up to this, I find it extraordinary that there are issues here of which until now I have had absolutely no knowledge. My feeling is that the majority of native Britons will share this reaction.

It has long been clear that this country's occupation of India was an unholy alliance between state and church. The state, Great Britain, in pursuit of international standing absurdly out of proportion to its own size and the massive material advantages that went with it. The Church, Christianity, which had perverted the simple message of its founder and believed it could justify imposing its own version on a "primitive" people with a concept of original sin and the claim that it alone possessed the means to personal salvation. Between them they were able to devise an extraordinarily successful divide-and-rule format which did immense damage to that country.

The tragedy seems to be that they chose to ignore the fact that they were working hand in hand to gain power over a nation whose spiritual tradition had already been in existence for three thousand years when Jesus Christ was born. A tradition, moreover, based on the direct religious experiences of its founders, rather than the man-made tenets of a self-serving priesthood.

The class system already so successful in Great Britain (and still firmly in place to this day) was the obvious model to achieve this end. But as I understand you, what I – and I believe many other people here – did <u>not</u> know was that in India before we arrived only a social system which defined people according to the work that they did, often passed on from father to son, was in existence. I had no idea that it was the British and its Church which turned these people into a criminal caste – and worse – one to which they were condemned from birth, with <u>no possibility of escape or redemption</u>. I had been led to believe that this appalling idea was something which the British inherited from the Indians themselves. As such, it has always been quoted as a major criticism of pre-colonial India, and by extension, as a justification of our time there. Against this, you refer to the absence of the word caste in Hindu scriptures... To learn what really lay behind the British Raj places a wholly different complexion on "the jewel in the crown."

Clearly, it seems to me you are right in demanding an apology for this disgraceful falsehood. And also such reparation as is possible at this distance in time for the damage it has caused – and is still causing to people both in India itself and among the Dharmic residents of this country. An amendment to the Act must, in addition, contain the clearest possible assurances that a continuation of any remnants of caste will be fully addressed by the legal system. This brings me to the question of your approach to this matter at this particular time.

The West, quite understandably despite all its statements about "the battle against terrorism," is now reaping the whirlwind for the sins of our fathers. We are seeing the collapse of our world on the same two fronts that brought about the exploitation of the Indian sub-continent, of Africa and everywhere else where the opportunity for material or religious gain could be seen. We have long had it coming, and now it has arrived. At this moment we are almost certainly closer to destroying the world than we have ever been. So far, we have been discussing fairly recent events which have helped to bring us to this point. The bigger picture, however, reveals a fundamental aberration regarding man's attitude to this universe and our purpose in being here.

As the founding fathers of the Hindu tradition – and others even before them – were aware, both man and his fellow sentient creatures are spiritual beings. But science, which set out to discover the mind of God, after early successes in explaining the workings of the universe, decided in its hubris that it no longer needed him, switching its focus to a purely material reality, a thing of chance mutation subject only to the prevailing environment as to what should and should not survive. And so began our descent into materialism from which all our problems stem.

I see our situation as a reflection not of gross human wickedness but of man's frailty in his role as the present cutting edge of progress. In a godless, purposeless creation of only material substance at the whim of chance mutation what else is there but every-man-for-himself and the pursuit of personal wealth? We have learned the hard way that if that really is how things are there is a heavy price to pay. Greed, the exploitation of the weakest, the widening gulf between the haves and have-nots lead to violence, mass rape and child-abuse and all the other horrors of which we now hear every single day. The result is that both our materialist science and Christianity in the perverted form in which it has come down to us are now both in their death throes.

Again, though surprised by the vehemence with which you express your feelings in regard to the treatment of your people, I must say again that I recognise that you appear to have right on your side. But it brings us to the living individuals against whom you are currently directing your attack. Yes, of course we collectively share the inherited responsibility for what the British did. Those personally responsible, however, are now long gone. The targets at which you are aiming are not those people themselves. I wonder, too, just how many of those on the receiving end of this attack are any more aware of the full background to the hate crimes to which you refer than I was. A number of the people you quote suggest that it is a large proportion. Unfortunately there is a great deal of repetition in your response to the Harries amendment. This has the effect of progressively reinforcing the sense of animosity that already pervades it.

Unlike the Jihad element of Islam, the Dharmic nations have not, thank God, descended into the extremes of mass killing and suicide bombers. You have so far retained the moral high ground, despite the high proportion you quote of racist threats, bullying and especially Islamophobic hate crimes directed against Hindus.

The West is at a crucial point in its history. Both the reductionist scientific method, which has sought to explain creation in purely material terms, and the perverted form of Christianity which has come down to us have each failed and are now in their death throes. But my intuition tells me that they are linked in a way which will soon bring about major changes for both. The key is the present state of physics, which I believe will now be forced to accept the existence of nonlocal mind. It is only this which will enable science to overcome the greatest challenge it has ever faced: the unification of general relativity and quantum mechanics. For almost a hundred years the two have seemed totally incompatible.

The acceptance of nonlocal mind will bring about immense changes. In science, it will open the door to a range of psychic human experiences which so far have been anathema to the materialist position. In the Christian religions, it will affect such issues as direct spiritual contact with the godhead and reincarnation, which have for so long been barriers to the reality of the cosmos. So I believe change is on the way, and the experiences which the Dharmic traditions have accepted for so long will be an important part of it.

Which brings me back to that Sunday morning and the television programme "The Big Questions" when I first saw you in action from your position on the moral high ground. As the spokesmen (and women) of the warring Christian factions were knocking seven bells out of one another, you sat quietly in the front row. When the chair-man finally came to you, suddenly here was a grown-up, talking real sense and from a much longer perspective, gently chiding them, but with humour and more in sorrow than anger.

In addition to his healing mission to the planet Earth, the man Jesus brought the message that the most important means of dealing with the ills of the aberrant creation into which we have got ourselves is forgiveness. Please forgive us now, so that we can move forward together.

Ends

Extract from Voice of Dalit International - Annual Accounts 2013-2014 Lambeth Palace meeting:

"Meetings with Lord Bishop Richard Harries and participation in the Church Urban Forum [CUF] conference on 'Poverty in London', wherein the ArchBishop of Canterbury was giving the keynote address, gave an opportunity for VODI to raise a criticism from the Dalit Diaspora Communities, who felt that despite living in a Christian country, the UK Church seemed inactive on the caste legislation issue. This led to a meeting for VODI and DSNUK representatives at Lambeth Palace, with Canon Toby Howorth, Inter - Religious Affairs. He said that unfortunately they did not have a Dalit Desk, that the Church of England [C of E] supports the caste legislation, which could be seen clearly through Bishop Lord Harries, one of the main persons driving the course of the legislation. Other C of E Bishops were also there in the House of Lords. VODI suggested that the Hindu section of the Dalit Diaspora communities be invited for the inter-faith meetings of the Hindu and Christian organisations. Canon Howorth said that if caste was put on the agenda, the mainstream Hindu representatives who refused to discuss it, would not attend. However he said he would raise the concerns of the Diaspora communities to the ArchBishop, that it seemed that the Church was not active enough on the caste issue and see what more could be done."

Pt Satish K. Sharma

National Council of Hindu Temples UK (NCHT)
REGISTERED OFFICE: c/o SHREE SANATAN MANDIR,
84 WEYMOUTH STREET, OFF CATHERINE STREET, LEICESTER, LE4 6FQ

Tel: 01162661402   **Email: info@nchtuk.org**   **Website: www.nchtuk.org**

16th May 2013

Attn: Richard Atkinson, Bishop of Bedford (by email)

Dear Richard,

Lord Harries and the Caste Crusade

I thank the Christian members of the Hindu Christian Forum for gathering together to give consideration to the issue of Lord Harries and the devastating effect of his interference in the affairs of the British Hindu community.

I reminded the meeting of Archbishop Rowan's statement at the founding of the Hindu Christian forum "We have been warned. We warn one another yet again of supposing too soon that we understand everything about each other. God forbid that we should think that. If we understood each other perfectly there would be no work to do, and no surprises, and no excitement". Recent experience of this discriminatory Anti Hindu legislation, which has been rushed through by Lord Harries, with out the Christian members of the HCF having been consulted, is testament to how much work still needs to be done. At this present moment we British Hindu's have had enough surprises and excitement.

I advised the gathering of a simple question which was troubling the Hindu community, which was this:- **"We wish to know whether Lord Harries' actions were bumbling incompetence of the highest order or whether they were based upon malice towards the British Hindu Community".**

Having reviewed his actions and his rhetoric and the outcome of his initiative, I, along with every other person who has calmly conducted the same analysis, have arrived at a conclusion which gives rise to the gravest of concerns regarding the evidently racist nature of all of the Lord's who have so eloquently risen to supposedly stand in defence of the British principle of rooting out Discrimination in all of its forms.

On behalf of the Hindu community, I as the NCHT Hindu member of the HCF and Sanjay Jagatia, representative of the AHO, presented to you publically available evidence and the ensuing reasoning which brought us to the undesirable conclusion that Lord Harries ▓▓▓▓▓▓▓ was guilty of Inciting religious hatred of Hindus and we came seeking clarification of the formal British Christian position. Privately, our greatest fear was that this Racism which seems to have presently manifested itself in an Anti Hindu form, may have spread its evil tendrils beyond the House of Lords and we also came seeking reassurance that the HCF was not an active participant on the assault which has been perpetrated upon our community.

Gauri Dasji from ISKCON and founding member of AHO, emphasised the severity of the issue and the need for the Forum to fulfil its purpose of receiving sensitive issues and as a gathering of spiritual practitioners, recognising hurt and participating in an urgent process of healing.

Having aired and explored the issues "passionately", my recollection of the responses of the Christian members of the Forum, to the request for a statement regarding Lord Harries's actions and behaviour were as follows:-

Established: July 1978   Charity Registration No.280718   Registered Office: Shree Sanatan Mandir, Leicester

"Caste, Conversion, A Colonial Conspiracy"

Contd.,

i) Joy gently stated that my stark statement that it was only 1 of 2 possibilities, either incompetence or Anti Hindu racism, was not necessarily appropriate and there could be other possibilities and this was accepted. A third alternative interpretation was however not presented.

ii) "Lord Harries doesn't in any way represent the Christian establishment" was submitted and supported by mention of his being a retired bishop and similar remarks which sought to gently distance the Christian members present from being judged by his actions and we Hindu's welcomed and accepted this as being a natural unstated recognition of the fact that he had had indeed committed a wrong. Otherwise why seek to create distance, perfectly reasonable.

iii) In response to Gauri Dasji's request for a public statement to that effect, confirming that this would result in a significant advance in restoring the damaged credibility of the Hindu Christian relationship, a tangible closing of ranks occurred culminating in a remark that it would be "difficult" for the Christian group to publicly criticise a fellow Christian and that Hindu's should communicate to their constituents that, privately the Christian contingent felt their hurt and recognised the harm, but publically they were not able to do this. Personally I was rendered speechless for a moment and I did declare that had a representative of the Hindu tradition incited such religious hatred, I as a Hindu, would have no qualms about demanding a public apology and that this position was disappointing. If a person molests a second person, a public recognition of the harm from the perpetrators family is a welcome balm to assuage hurt. Communicating such acknowledgement privately and asking the victim to circulate the private acknowledgement, thereby preserving the perpetrators family's public persona, is disingenuous at best. The reputation and standing of the British Hindu community was publically assaulted and tarnished in the Chamber of the House of Lords, its difficult to imagine greater humiliation – a private acknowledgement is hardly adequate recognition.

iv) Sanjayji asked the group as to whether they were aware of the last time a Christian Lord had presented a faith related amendment to Law, none could recall and Sanjayji advised that we had researched back as far as possible and found no trace – so why the urgency and rush to legislate and why on such an obviously Anti-Hindu platform?

v) After an initial suggestion that the Forum would need to retire and reflect and consider the issue before responding, the forum recognised Sanjayji's assertion that time was a constraint and a consensus emerged that the Forum would move towards writing to the relevant Ministers and emphasising that it was clear that the evidence upon which this amendment had been passed was insufficient and that genuine consultation and understanding of this issue was critical for Community Cohesion and that this would be done with all due haste.

Ministers from both parties have clearly stated that **caste is not "religion nor race specific"** and since this is a self evident truth, which "post legislation" has been trumpeted by all and sundry, including Lord Harries himself, we have a question to ask and this gives us great cause for concern as to the motives behind this issue and to the genuine honesty of those who so easily take the moral high ground on the issue of discrimination and the question is simply this. If this amendment is about rooting out Discrimination and "even one case of discrimination is one too many" and caste is so self evidently **"not religion nor race specific"** please, please someone tell the Hindu Community why ALL of the people in the NIESR report which the Lords have so loudly declared as a wonderful unimpeachable piece of research are **EXCLUSIVELY BROWN INDIANS"**? And why the anti Hindu rhetoric in the House?

Our greatest concern however is not to do with only these Lords against whom the volume of evidence is already irrefutable, our greater concern can simply be articulated in this question.

"Why is it that no Minister, no MP, no Christian, no civil servant, no legislator, no political commentator has even NOTICED that the NIESR report has a sample of ONLY BROWN INDIANS ? " No-one present at the meeting yesterday had even noticed either, we "brown Indians" couldn't help but notice yet another instance of racial discrimination.

Rowan Williams stated: "But the Mahatma is a very interesting example of someone who, as it were, reflects back to the Christian Church the riches and the challenges that the Christian Church itself doesn't fully appreciate. **He was able to say to his Christian friends, you don't really take seriously the Sermon on the Mount; you don't really take seriously the person whose name you bear and whose allegiance you claim. That is something Christians need to hear."**

We British Hindus, humbly recognising our own fallibility, remind you, our brothers and sisters in the service of Divinity, of your Christian scriptures, confident that you will act in the tradition of the Spirit of the one whose name your tradition bears:- "Thou shalt not bear false witness" and most relevantly Matthew 7.16 "By their fruits shall you know them". By your actions in response to the above question, we and everyone else whose eyes are on this issue, shall again recognise you. We look forward to a public statement from the Christian establishment, in response to the above very simple question.

Yours sincerely
On behalf of the NCHTUK

Satish K Sharma
General Secretary (Acting)

Established: July 1978   Charity Registration No.280718   Registered Office: Shree Sanatan Mandir. Leicester

102

Pt Satish K. Sharma

National Council of Hindu Temples UK (NCHT)
REGISTERED OFFICE: c/o SHREE SANATAN MANDIR,
84 WEYMOUTH STREET, OFF CATHERINE STREET, LEICESTER, LE4 6FQ

Tel: 01162661402   **Email: info@nchtuk.org**   **Website: www.nchtuk.org**

6th May 2013

Attn: Dr Kate Wharton, Lambeth Palace. (by email)

Dear Dr Wharton,

Lord Harries and the Caste Crusade

Thank you for the invitation to participate in what I hope will be a genuine and frank
exploration of this issue, courageously open to the recognition of the ugly factors which have
dominated the stage so far.

I am attaching a report which has been sent to Minister Helen Grant, as the first step in the
NCHT UK's process of "consultative engagement". This covers issues which I hope members of
the Hindu Christian Forum will find of interest and relevance and which we feel are at the heart
of the integrity of the Forum.

Core to the issue is the performance of Lord Harries http://www.youtube.com/watch?v=z5-
XQdinqHo , followed by the complete silence and tacit approval of the Christian members of the
InterFaith Community. By the time the Christian fundamentalist cleric, Lord Harries and his non
Hindu cohorts had concluded their masterclass in inciting religious hatred, half of the 800,000
British Hindus who are "non-Dalits", had been successfully portrayed as "dowry grabbing
female foetus killers".

According to the "statistics/facts" so skilfully mis-presented by the Honourable Lords, more
than half of all British Hindus are Caste Racists and by inference that means that half of our
mothers and daughters are Caste racists, half of every congregation in every Hindu Temple is
guilty of Caste discrimination, half of our Doctors and Accountants, Dentists and Lawyers are
rabid Caste Racists, half of the Hindu's in any gathering or grouping are Caste racists. We are
giving most serious consideration to the manner in which certain members of the House of
Lords "mis-represented" statistics and abused the protection of Parliamentary Privilege to
ferment and incite a wave of religious hatred towards the British Hindu community.

Now that the circus which took over the House of Lords "has left town", the truth about the
scale of this manipulation is becoming apparent and clearly visible to a much wider audience,
not just us members of the British Hindu Community at whom this act of malice was directed. I
recall clearly the manner in which Labour Prime Minister Tony Blair whipped up hysteria
regarding the Iraq War, daily chanting the "Weapons of Mass Destruction" mantra, claiming
that 45 minutes was all that stood behind us British Citizens and annihilation at the hands of the
Iraqi's war machine. I recall how the Labour government took up the chant and how MP's leapt
on to the bandwagon and not unsurprisingly, our elected representatives did the same in this
instance, led by "Bandwagon Barry" Gardiner, the elected representative and bosom friend of
the Hindu's of Brent. What happened to consulting those self same Hindu's who perennially
welcomed and garlanded these representatives at so many social and religious functions? It
would seem that when Lord Harries played his Pied Pipers pipe of Prejudice, the rats came
running. **The same question will be asked of ALL LABOUR MP's who seemed to think that
rushing to legislate was such a vitally necessary act, without thinking for a moment to check
the data, to perform even a cursory impact assessment, conduct consultation with grass roots
and to ask the Hindu organisations for their experience and input.**
Contd.,

Established: July 1978   Charity Registration No.280718   Registered Office: Shree Sanatan Mandir, Leicester

"Caste, Conversion, A Colonial Conspiracy"

Contd.,

Recent history, as clearly established by the Iraqi WMD issue (when the British nation was plunged into a war resulting in 179 British troop deaths and 100,000's of Iraqi deaths and NOT a single WMD discovered,) initiated by Labour's inflamatory rhetoric, highlights the tragically human susceptibility of our elected REPRESENTATIVES to unsubstantiated, unevidenced emotional verbiage and the Peers demonstrated their peerless skill in this area, with talk of **480,000 sufferers, 400 COMMUNITY LEADERS at the gates of the House** etc etc. and that vulnerability is something to be addressed in a different place. However in the InterFaith arena, we expected a completely different response from the Hindu Christian grass roots relationship and here we British Hindu's have been shown to have been again overly optimistic, as is our nature. We members of this 800,000 British Hindu community were expecting a wave of support from our fellows in the InterFaith community but almost as devastating as the hate filled invective has been the complete silence from the Christian Inter Faith quarter. It is clear that Hindu Christian dialogue in this country was perhaps not what we British Hindus naively assumed and I am disappointed that our "relationship" will need to be re-assessed in the light of this evidence.

Ministers from both parties have clearly stated that **caste is not "religion specific"**. **Secretary of State Maria Miller** writing to all MP's on the 25th April stated **"there is very little evidence of caste discrimination in Britain"** and yet Lord's Harries, Alton, Avebury, Cormack and Deben repeated that 400,000 of Her Majesty's HINDU subjects are affected by this terrible scourge and these Honourable Lords do not appear to be arithmetically challenged. So the two questions remains, "Why would the Lords so attack the British Hindu Community" and "Why have no Christians spoken out against such flagrant religious discrimination?". Do feelings of fraternity extend no further than Diwali greetings?

The unrelenting tirades against British Hindus will not now so easily be set aside. The volley of anti Hindu comments are still reverberating in the ears of British Hindu's and it has been clearly portrayed that here in the 21st century, in the "Mother of Parliaments", religious hatred against Hindus is perfectly acceptable, as long as it hides under the protective mantle of Parliamentary Privilege. We would ask those, such as Lord Harries who so brazenly brandish their religious credentials to reflect on how they have actually applied those Christian principles during the course of this debate and political process. Or is it simply yet another case of Christ saying one thing and the Church saying another?

Please extend my congratulations to Lord Harries, since introducing his amendment, the British legal profession is happily chattering away about the issue of caste being a "British Hindu" problem (refer below), as we Hindu's feared they would and you will see from the email attached below, UK Hindu's are now in conflict with UK Hindu's and any British born Hindu who has the misfortune of having ancestors who were branded "not low caste" by the 1871 British Colonial census, is now automatically required to defend him/herself against allegations of assumed guilt. **We did warn legislators and our warnings fell on deaf ears**. We compliment the Honourable Lord and all who supported him in this assault on British Hindus for successfully manipulating and misleading the whole of the Parliamentary machinery so skilfully.

In conclusion, the members of the NCHTUK would be grateful to hear "Archbishop Justin's" position on this issue and we would be grateful if you could bring this matter to his urgent attention. As of yet we are not convinced about this strange, seemingly irrational approach which prefers to "legislate first and consult later" or "Publicise first and dialogue second", so we shall hope for a response from the Archbishop in the very near future, prior to publishing the details of our letter to our Member Temples and wider Hindu Community. Having said that we shall be presenting the video of the House of Lords to our Hindu community Leaders (not quite 400 but possibly a humble and totally legitimate 40/50 representing at **least** 35,000 Hindus) on Wednesday evening and should they feel that this issue should be immediately shared, we will have to give consideration to their wishes irrespective of the Archbishops response or not.

With regard to the possibility of a Hindu Christian Forum "round table", we would submit that there is a significant amount of work to do before this is appropriate, certainly before we can all sit around the same table as friends sharing food and experiences. After all according to the Honourable Christian Lords, half of the Hindus around that table would be caste racists.

Yours sincerely
On behalf of the NCHTUK

Satish

Satish K Sharma
General Secretary (Acting)
www.nchtuk.org

Contd

Established: July 1978   Charity Registration No.280718   Registered Office: Shree Sanatan Mandir, Leicester

contd.,

Lord Harries Objective 2 Achieved and initiated
Outside the Ivory towers of Parliament, where Ministers and Hansard record that "Caste is not specific to one Religion or Culture" in the court of public opinion, **CASTE DISCRIMINATION CLEARLY ESTABLISHED AS A SIGNIFICANT BRITISH HINDU PROBLEM**.

http://employmentlawblog.ffw.com/2013/caste-discrimination-to-be-outlawed-in-uk
http://www.moonbeever.com/category-blog-entry/582-equality-act-ii-the-question-of-caste

A simple search on Google under "Caste legislation" generates a plethora of "professionals" giving their opinion on the now exclusively Hindu problem of Caste. How is this incalculable harm to be repaired or even to be countered?

Printed in Great Britain
by Amazon